SANDCASTLES

TEXT BY JOSEPH ALLEN
DESIGNED BY
DON & DEBRA McQUISTON
PHOTOGRAPHY BY
MARSHALL HARRINGTON

SANDCASTLES
THE SPLENDORS OF ENCHANTMENT

A Dolphin Book   Doubleday & Company, Inc.   Garden City, New York   1981

Library of Congress Cataloging in Publication Data

Allen, Joseph, 1944–
    Sandcastles.

    1.   Sand craft.   2.   Sandcastles.
3.   Sand sculpture.   I.   Title.
TT865.A43   736′.9   80-1648
ISBN 0-385-15931-5

This book is dedicated to
The Sandcastlers of the World
without whose imaginations
nothing could have happened
and to
The International Castles-Institute
H.S.H. Franz Josef II, Sovereign
Prince of Liechtenstein, Patron
The Marquis de Amodio, President
H.S.H. The Princess zu Bentheim-
Tecklenburg, Vice President

FOREWORD

The International Castles-Institute, as the World Federation of Castles and Historic Houses, preserves this priceless heritage for future generations and also stimulates the public's interest in its survival. Therefore, as the International Castles-Institute's President, I am both proud and pleased to congratulate and encourage *Sandcastles* on its outstanding success. The scale models found in *Sandcastles*, though ephemeral when compared to the perenniality of their originals, nevertheless contribute in making better known the splendours of these castles.

I hope that this book will yet further the defence of these masterpieces and I wish every success to all those who have made it possible, trusting that it will induce its readers to support the International Castles-Institute's efforts.

The Marquis de Amodio, O.B.E.
President
International Castles-Institute
World Federation for the
Protection of Historic Castles and
Country Houses with Consultative
Status at the Council of Europe
and at UNESCO

AUTHOR'S NOTE

Why a book on sandcastles? It's difficult to lay a finger on just what the appeal of these ephemeral masterpieces is. Not that there is any doubt about their ability to fascinate; a major sandcastle can easily draw ten thousand spectators.

My own interest in sandcastles has sprung from a dilemma inherent in sand. It's so easy to work, to pile up, to carve. There's no resistance to it; one doesn't need the patience of a woodcarver or a stonemason. On the other hand, the life-span is so short that I have barely time to admire them before they're gone. The line between satisfaction and sadness is thin indeed.

Anyone who has ever played on a beach with children knows the poignancy of sandcastles. Like the children themselves, they are the essence of innocence. And like the fleeting moments of childhood, they are gone almost before you finish smiling at them.

The magnificent sandcastles and sand creatures you will see in this book were culled from literally hundreds of contest entries and specially commissioned projects. In selecting these, we had to reject others. It was a painful process; we loved those that we kept, but we hated to lose the ones we had to cut.

It allowed me, as no other subject could, to indulge in daydreams, to write on what seems, in retrospect, to have been an astonishing array of subjects. All the romance and adventure that has held over from my own childhood was unleashed (even encouraged). But it would be folly to suggest that I could have kept my long-restrained child-self in check alone. That this book has been published is a tribute to the editors of Dolphin/Doubleday, to whom we owe our thanks. We want particularly to mention the kind offices of Mr. Barry Lippman, whose help has been invaluable.

We have been fortunate since the early days of *Sandcastles* to enjoy the enthusiastic support and encouragement of the International Castles-Institute, an organization dedicated to the preservation of the castle heritage, with consultative status at UNESCO and the Council of Europe. We wish to acknowledge the debt we owe particularly to the Marquis de Amodio, and to His Serene Highness, the Sovereign Prince of Liechtenstien. They are, respectively, the President and the Patron of the Institute.

But this book would have not been possible, could have never been started, without the assistance freely offered to us by the spectacularly gifted sandcastlers themselves. We could not possibly name the builders of each and every castle in the book, but there are certain sand artists without whose names these acknowledgements would be painfully incomplete:

Joseph Alldredge, Richard Carter, Gary Kinsella and Sand Castling Inc., Norman Kraus, John Laver, Diane Lewis, Duncan McArthur, Brian O'Hara, Gregory L. O'Laughlin, Jerry Quell, Lita Reynolds, Beth Runner, Nancy Samuelsen, Judith Shoup, Mike Stewart and Todd Vanderpluym.

Sandcastles has been a mutual effort from the beginning, the kind of project I have always wanted to work on. The visual sensitivity of Marshall Harrington, the delicate and imaginative designs of Debra and Don McQuiston, and my own text—all have been enriched by the stimulating interchange of ideas we found (miraculously) possible.

We join together in wishing you brilliant sandcastles, the splendors of your own enchanted imagination.

CONTENTS

1

Crossing the Drawbridge

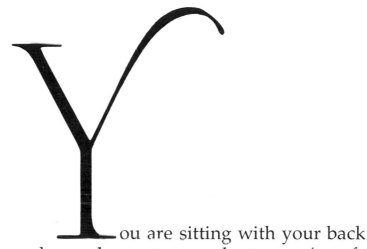

You are sitting with your back to the land, sitting hunched over, knees drawn to your chest, your bare feet half buried in white sand.

Now look across the water at the silver glare that dances across the surface of the waves. As you gaze, imagine that the light you see is the shimmering glint of an age long past.

The foam of the waves pounds the shore like a team of white steeds from a fairy-tale kingdom under the sea. Look! Can you see a knight? an ethereal horseman? a shining cavalier?

His horse is draped in brightly colored silks: yellow, orange, red. His body is encased in silver armor. Plumes decorate his helmet and a white crusader's tunic covers his torso, emblazoned with a scarlet Maltese cross.

He might be Lancelot. He might be Roland, or Tancredi, or the Black Prince. He might be Sir Gawain in eternal quest of the Grail, or Sir Tristan galloping to his love. But with a single glimpse, he is gone, fading back into the tide.

The next day, when the sun is on your back, and the world is behind you, you dig your hands into the sand and let it dribble out between your fingers. It forms a tiny hillock: perhaps the beginning of a modest sand castle. The sand feels good. It invites you to squeeze it, mold it. You begin idly to pile up a shapeless mound and pat it down. You keep glancing up at the waves to see if your vision has returned, but the sun's light flashes formlessly and sends you back to the sand.

There, with your mind freed from the demands of the civilized world, the sand beckons your imagination with offers of enchantment, of spells, of magic. Filled with the power of imagination, a person can turn a vision into reality.

The cloud-capped towers of Byzantium are within reach, the gorgeous palaces of divine monarchs, the solemn temples of antiquity. The great globe itself will change at your touch, transforming itself into whatever magical milieu you summon.

In such a situation the beach can become a land from faraway times. As with movies, absolutely anything can happen. The horseman from the sea can clamber onto dry land.

Call forth from the ocean air the bright pennants of the Field of the Cloth of Gold, the gilded pavilions of Samarkand, the heroes of the Age of Chivalry.

Summon to your presence the great lovers of the Age of Romance. Weep for Heloise and Abelard, the favorite tragedy of the Middle Ages—she a pious nun, he a proud academician mutilated by her vengeful family after he dared make love to her. Groan with the inevitable fates of Guinevere and Lancelot, as they bring Camelot crashing down about their heads and give the world over to chaos with the death of Arthur. Look benevolently on Fair Rosamund and her lover, King Henry II, and feel the stabbing heartbreak of Henry's grief when his queen poisons his love in her garden bower.

Shaping and sculpting the sand around you, you will be able to rebuild the great white walls and towering citadels of the Age of Castles. You will be able to experience the glory and pageantry of an age forever gone.

These times are the thousand years of the Middle Ages, from the fall of Rome to the flowering of the Renaissance. The millennium from 500 to 1500 AD was filled with violence, with love and breathless passion, with discovery, faith, laughter, holiness, adventure, and

nobility. From the Viking invasions to the discovery of America, the Middle Ages was the time that gave Europe its character, its history, and its nationalities.

Re-create for yourself the fascination of the millions of Europeans who stared in wonder at the new symbol the Crusaders brought home from the deserts of the Middle East: the rose. Its flowery perfection was thought to be the fairest representation of the Queen of Heaven—and its image appears in stained glass on the walls of the great Gothic cathedrals dedicated to her. That stained glass was made from the same beach sand you can now form into a very special type of reality that balances on the borders of fantasy.

As you read through the chapters of this book, you will see amazing possibilities heave into life. You will see formless, shapeless sand become the landscapes of dreams. Dragons will live again. And if you watch closely you will experience mortality; you will know the meaning of destruction—and its inevitability.

The story is told that King Cnut, the Danish emperor whose lands included what we now know as England, was thought by his people to be the most powerful man in the world: almost a god. He set up a famous experiment to prove his own mortality. He had his throne carried in pomp to one of the rocky beaches of East Anglia and set up at the tide line. Then, with his whole court in attendance, he stood facing the ocean and commanded the tide to stop. It did not, and before long he was standing waist deep in water. His point was made.

And so it is with sand fantasy. The gilded towers can be built by force of will and power of imagination, but they cannot be protected from the onrush of the tidal marauders. Sand fantasies are doomed from their beginnings to absolute mortality—to death, to destruction, to oblivion.

It is as inevitable as the rising sun. The ocean will gather its forces, rolling in a great single line, a battle formation as old as the earth itself: waves. They sweep across the oceans of the world, gathering power.

And one wave will reach beyond all the others—as greedy and unfeeling as all the Alexanders, the Tamerlanes, the Napoleons of history. And that one wave will turn the bright day of your imagination into just another dusk on the beach.

Some of the greatest moments of history have been times of unspeakable loss. But, oh, for one brief, shining moment. . . .

Saint George Slaying the Dragon. In the feudal period, the world of beasts, demons, and monsters was an article of faith. Satan could — and did — appear in thousands of horrible guises. It took a knight of exceptional holiness and courage to face off the Devil himself. Saint George has always been the perfect cavalier, the shining white knight, the angelic foille to pierce the Heart of Darkness.

Although he may have never lived, Saint George figures in the mythology of virtually every nation of Europe. He is the patron saint of England and of Holy Russia. His name means "nobility" in Greek. He was the promise of salvation to generations of medieval children brought up on tales of Hell and of the leering Evil One.

2

Seven Surviving Castles

The age of castle-building is gone and the great castle builders are all long dead. The world is dotted with the magnificent products of their labors—some surviving in all their fierce majesty, others slowly decaying and collapsing.

The process of attrition in castles is caused by two principal factors: people and time. Some of the greatest castles, for instance, did not survive the periods in which they were built. Richard the Lion-Hearted's pride, Château Gaillard, did not survive more than fifteen years longer than Richard himself; the French sacked and destroyed it. John of Gaunt's legendary Palace of the Savoy, which was spoken of as the most magnificent castle in the world, was burned to the ground by a London mob before John himself died. All but one of the famed Rhinecastles lie in ruins, staring down at the river, specters of a civilization long absent.

But other castles seem to live a charmed existence. Wars have raged all around them—even within them. They survive devastating earthquakes, centuries of neglect, the predations of tourists and souvenir hunters, as though a powerful wizard kept watch over them. In this chapter we are going to have a look at some of these hardy survivors. We'll learn how and why they were built, the stories they have beheld, the myths and legends that have grown up about them.

We have chosen the castles for this chapter from a world castle heritage that is still large. We have chosen a group of castles that represents thirteen centuries of castle-building, from Castel Sant' Angelo in Rome, which was begun by the Roman emperor Hadrian as a mausoleum in 135 AD, to the more recent citadels: the Kremlin, Bran Castle, and the reconstructed Windsor Castle.

All these castles were used for centuries as fortified homes. Some were the royal homes of powerful monarchs, and some were the imperial residences of emperors and czars. Others were the residences of great nobles, notorious villains, and pious monks.

Castles are repositories of great romance, of fantastic lies, of hideous murders, of enduring love stories. In this chapter you will meet people as diverse as Queen Victoria, King Edward the Confessor, and Count Dracula. Their common link is that they belong to a very small and special group of people: the great, the powerful, the castle dwellers.

Castel Sant' Angelo

By far the senior member of our august group of survivors is the Pope's citadel in Rome, Castel Sant' Angelo. It stands next to the Tiber River, guarding the approach to the Seven Hills of Rome, just as it has stood for more than 1,800 years.

Castel Sant' Angelo has been a silent sentinel through more history than a single mind can easily grasp. When the far-flung Roman Empire saw its blazing zenith of world domination,

Castel Saint' Angelo was there.

It witnessed successive invasions of the Eternal City by Celts, Vandals, Goths and Visigoths, Lombards, and Germans. It stood through the execution of the last emperor of the West, Romulus Augustulus, during the plunder of Rome in the dark year, 476 AD. And in that faraway past, Castel Sant' Angelo was already older than any public building in North America is today.

Through the Dark Ages, the building which had begun as a house of death—it was built as a mausoleum for the Emperor Hadrian in 135 AD—became a notorious house of torture and oblivion. It was a bastion of Roman revenge and vendetta, a prison that swallowed members of the great feuding families of Italy.

But despite its dark history, Hadrian's Tomb survived. While the Coliseum decayed and collapsed; while the Forum disappeared into the palazzi of Rome; while Nero's Golden Palace was razed to bare earth—Hadrian's Tomb survived. And in the Middle

Ages it experienced a totally unexpected renaissance when it became Castel Sant' Angelo, fortress of the capital of Christianity.

According to the medieval Italians, this unexpected conversion occurred as a result of a spectacular miracle. The early fourteenth century was a time of war and pestilence in Europe. And it was, particularly, the time of the Black Death.

The Black Death, or bubonic plague, killed as much as half the population of Europe in a most grisly fashion. It hit cities particularly hard, decimating the great capitals and trade centers. As we now know, it was carried by the fleas of brown rats. Its victims rarely recovered once infected, but died of symptoms which included high fevers, chills, boils, vomiting, and dysentery.

Rome was hard hit. The people died faster than they could be buried, and enormous funeral pyres lighted the skies of the city nightly. At the height of the horror, a blaze of heavenly fire

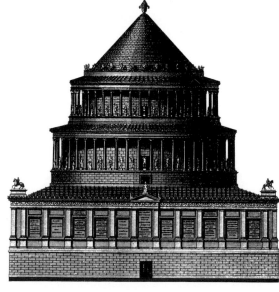

Hadrian was an emperor who left monuments behind. The wall he built across the northern border of England still stands, although 1800 years of invasion and war have almost reduced it to ruins.

His family tomb was designed

to outdo the Mausoleum at Halicarnassus, considered then to be one of the wonders of the world — a fit companion to the great pyramids of Egypt. It was then a model of Hellenistic symmetry. Today's Castel Sant' Angelo is an expansion of the tomb into a grander design.

eclipsed the cremation fires as it spun down toward earth.

According to Roman tradition, that blaze of light was none other than God's messenger, the Archangel Michael. Whoever or whatever it was, it came to rest on the pinnacle of Hadrian's Tomb. And thus was Rome delivered from the Black Death, which disappeared from Rome immediately, never to return.

Shortly thereafter, Hadrian's Tomb became known as Castel Sant' Angelo, or "The Castle of the Holy Angel." Soon a heroic statue of the flaming angel was raised on the highest point of the castle, sword aloft, gigantic wings outspread over his beloved city. And there that angel has remained to this day.

But the history of Castel Sant' Angelo was even then far from finished. Indeed its most historic event had yet to happen, although it was not far off.

The year 1527 was a tumultuous one all over Europe. The brash and brilliant young king of England, Henry VIII, had decided that he

wanted to divorce his Spanish queen, Catherine of Aragon. The ultimate result of that decision was the conversion of Britain to Protestantism, and the alienation of the British monarchy from the states of Europe. But while Henry was busy seducing his feisty mistress, Anne Boleyn, more violent events were engulfing Italy.

The Holy Roman Emperor was, in his own way, settling a grievance with the papacy. Since the time of Charlemagne, the popes had been autonomous rulers of a conglomeration called the Papal States. The rest of Italy had had a checkered history, but generally the northern part had

been a province of the Holy Roman Empire, while the south had been variously under the control of the Norman dukes, the Spanish kings, and the French crown. The balance of power between the holy Roman Emperors and the French kings seemed to depend on the direction the pope leaned. The Vicar of Christ at that time was an illegitimate son of Lorenzo the Magnificent, and had all the devious blood of the de Medici. His name was Giulio de Medici, and he took the papal name of Clement VII. Clement VII made the mistake of deciding in favor of the king of France.

The Emperor Charles V was enraged, so enraged that he ordered his troops to attack the city of Rome—an act that had no precedent in Christian annals. Rome had always been a sacred city, at least physically. Armies had camped on its outskirts, but had never invaded it.

Charles V's troops were mostly Lutheran and possessed the reforming zeal that Martin

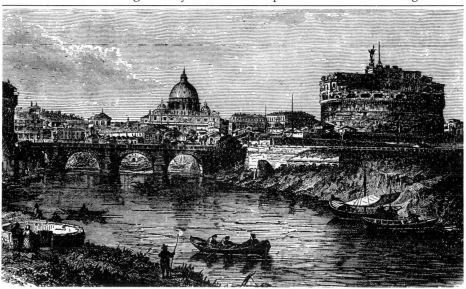

Castel Sant' Angelo as it has appeared for the last 1000 years or so. The bridge that spans the Tiber in front of it, the Pons Aelius, predates the castle by a year; it was completed in 134 AD.

By turns a fortress, a prison, a chamber of torture, a holy edifice, and a palace of popes, Castel Sant' Angelo figures prominently in the history of the Eternal City. During the Black Death in the fourteenth century, the Archangel Michael is said to have appeared on its pinnacle as a ball of fire and saved the city from the pestilence.

In the years immediately following the French Revolution, the aristocracy of Italy used Sant' Angelo as its bastion of terror in Rome. Victorien Sardou's masterpiece of melodrama, *La Tosca*, sets its last act here — where the heroine catapults herself off the walls into the river. It was in performing *La Tosca* that Sarah Bernhardt broke a leg that later had to be amputated. Her career gained in brilliance even after she lost her leg, and the theatrical "Break a leg!" thereafter became a byword for great performing luck.

Today's Castel Sant' Angelo is an official papal residence, as it has been for centuries. It also houses the Italian headquarters of the International Castles-Institute.

Luther had preached in their hometowns. They nearly destroyed the city in their frenzy. The Vatican and St. Peter's Basilica were looted and used as stables and brothels. The art treasures of the city were broken, burned, and stolen. The women of the city were raped and butchered. Mayhem held full sway. The terrified pope barricaded himself inside Castel Sant' Angelo.

Such was the moment when Henry VIII's envoy arrived to ask for Henry's divorce from the emperor's niece, Catherine. It did not seem wise to Clement to grant such a divorce just at that moment, with the emperor's madmen frothing and screaming outside his doors.

Clement spent six months locked inside Sant' Angelo, and Sant' Angelo was the only building in Rome that escaped the looting and pillaging of the emperor's troops. As such it proved to be the salvation of the greatest Vatican art treasures. Because, unknown to the emperor, the Vatican had been connected to Castel Sant' Angelo by a mile-long underground tunnel. And the holiest and most valuable Vatican possessions were evacuated via that catacomblike viaduct.

Various other occupants of Sant' Angelo have made various additions and alterations since the time of Clement VII, but the basic structure of Hadrian's Tomb remains. It crouches behind the Pons Aelius, a bridge that predates even Sant' Angelo itself, blessed by the angelic messenger of God, awaiting its next time of need. Popes have come and gone since then; all have spent time in Sant' Angelo. With the whittling down of the Papal States to the grounds of the Vatican City, Castel Sant' Angelo and Castel Gondolfo in the mountains behind Rome remain the only papal real estate left to the Roman pontiffs.

Sand gives Castel Sant' Angelo the mystical surrealism that everyday Roman traffic cannot supply.

The ghosts of centuries would feel at home in this towering replica of the ancient original.

The glistening sun casts a spell over the sand, and the marauding waters of the ocean have washed rivulets in the sandy would-be Tiber.

Several great angels have, in turn, surmounted the Castel. They

have perished in earthquakes, fires, wars, and mob fervor. The white figure that crowns today's Sant' Angelo may one day erode into the faceless winged creature sculpted here from sand.

The evenly

spaced crenelations and corbels are a masterpiece of planning and measurement. They are calculated to give the impression of a double-toothed parapet: two corbels to one crenel.

One of the world's most widely recognized landmarks, Mont Saint Michel has persevered in Gothic splendor for over 900 years. Like a real sandcastle, it is entirely surrounded by the sea at high tide.

Gothic arches with the distinctive pointed cap are the hallmark of the best medieval architecture. This cloister (*opposite*) at Mont Saint Michel belies an admiration for the finest in Arab architecture as well. With a little imagination, it could be the Alhambra.

Mont Saint Michel

By strange coincidence, the second castle we have chosen to profile is named after the same archangel who is the patron of Castel Sant' Angelo in Rome: St. Michael, who cast Lucifer out of Heaven.

But the locale is far removed from Rome. This time we are on the coast of Normandy, a bewitchingly beautiful seascape. As we gaze at the choppy waters north of us, we know that the south coast of England hovers enticingly just beyond sight.

Mont Saint Michel is one of the most famous tourist spots in the world. Aside from Paris itself, Mont Saint Michel is the best-known place in France—the subject of innumerable travel posters and photographs. Its full name is Mont Saint Michel au Peril de la Mer, or "Saint Michael's Mount in Danger from the Sea." The name is not idly given.

As the world knows, this famous abbey and fortress is an offshore island at high tide and a contiguous part of the mainland at low tide. Many are the invaders who have drowned in the onrush of the protective tides at Mont Saint Michel. Today a long causeway connects the island with the mainland, so that it is accessible even when the waters surround it, but such has not always been the case.

Mont Saint Michel is more than 1,000 years old, and during that 1,000 years it has withstood not only the sea and nature, but military attacks, revolutions, fire, and desecration. Yet it survives.

It began, as far as historians can tell, with a church built on the island during the time of Charlemagne or of Alfred the Great, both of whom reigned over their kingdoms during the ninth century. It was a period of intellectual achievement in the two great courts; it was also the time of the bloodcurdling Viking invasions. The hulking, blond

Norsemen in their fierce longboats were the scourge of Europe from Romania in the east to Greenland or even America in the west. And they seemed to have no hint of mercy in them.

During the century after Alfred's death, the Viking hordes became omnipotent in the lands they chose to occupy. England was a private estate of Cnut, the Danish emperor. And the north coast of France was so completely inundated by Norsemen that it became known as Normandy, "the land of the Norsemen."

The most powerful Viking chieftains in northern France grabbed for themselves the title and lands that became the Duchy of Normandy, and they spawned some of history's most prodigious villains and heroes. The first was Richard Sans Peur (Richard the Fearless), who established the Norman Dukes' interest in the Archangel's Mountain.

In 966 AD, Richard Sans Peur did some monastic housecleaning. He pitched out the monks who had encamped on the island and invited a group of Italian Benedictines from Monte Cassino to take their place. The new inhabitants founded and built the spectacular church that still covers the entire top third of the island.

It was begun in 1020 by one Abbot Hildebert, a man of nearly insane architectural pretensions. He may have put his trust too entirely in the angelic patron of the spot. The Archangel's super-natural powers would have been needed to support the quixotic concept that Hildebert saw through to completion.

The abbot built his gargantuan church on an artificial platform perched on the topmost rock of the island—unwilling as he was to sacrifice even one foot of height. That topmost rock was a thin pinnacle thirty feet tall, but that did not daunt the ambitious abbot. He merely dictated that the abbey be constructed on a masonry foundation that extended down from the apex on all four sides of the church. The apex of that needle of rock is today the floor of the very center of the abbey: the intersection of the nave and the transept. But the abbey is no longer the showplace that Hilde-bert built.

Actually the abbey took on more grandeur than even Hildebert dreamt of. Two enormous Gothic towers were added after Hilde-bert's death. And then the whole thing started to collapse in the year 1300.

Meanwhile the Dukes of Normandy had created two of history's most unforgettable char-acters. One was the archfiend of the early Middle Ages: a blood-

thirsty, demonic, and vengeful maniac nicknamed Robert le Diable (Robert the Devil). The other was William the Bastard, later known to the world as William the Conqueror.

When William became Duke of Normandy, the blood of his Viking ancestors had not ceased to boil in his veins. He was at heart a seafarer and a plunderer, and he perched himself in Hildebert's abbey, which was conveniently turned at least partially into a palace for the new duke.

And from this rocky and im-pregnable fortress, he swooped down on the Channel to pick up a very impressive prisoner in the fatal year of 1058. It was the very year that Macbeth and his Lady murdered the King of Scotland, a year so singularly ill-favored by the stars. William's unwilling guest was a powerful Danish lord then resident in England: Harold Godwinson. William extracted a promise from Harold that when the current King of England should die, Harold would support

William's faint claim to the English throne. Harold repudiated the promise later and claimed the throne for himself as Harold II upon the death of Edward the Confessor, the last Anglo-Saxon king.

But the Bastard was not one to take a broken promise lightly. He waited for the feast of Michael the Archangel on October 16, in the year of Edward the Confessor's death. And then he crossed the Channel and altered the course of history. The year was 1066 AD, and William set up a new monarchy in England that has lasted until the present. Harold never had a chance to stop the Conqueror; he was killed by an arrow in the eye during the first battle at a place known as Hastings.

But its illustrious history did not keep the building from falling in on itself in 1618, when the entire front facade began to give way during the reign of Louis XIII and Cardinal Richelieu. There it sat for 158 years in a state of partial collapse. And in 1776 the entire facade and half the church was pulled down. What we see today is merely a shadow of the grandeur that was intended—and that lived for 400 years. But oh what a shadow!

The finest literary hero of the Middle Ages was Roland, whose exploits were sung by minstrels for half a millennium over the length and breadth of the known world. When Roland dies after the Battle of Roncesvalles, he is borne off to heaven by two figures: the angel Gabriel and an angel whom the poet calls "Seint Michiel de la mer del peril." The abbey and the angel had become one.

Abbot Hildebert's grandiose edifice may not survive intact in today's Mont Saint Michel, but the abbey/church that crowns this island remains one of the architectural wonders of France.

Robert le Diable and William the Conqueror lived here. Five hundred years of holy Benedictines prayed here before half the church collapsed in 1776.

The bourgeois of medieval Normandy would have no trouble finding his way home in this replica. The homes are the same; the sky is the same; the surrounding sand is the same. What is different? Certainly not the faith that built both, nor the sense of beauty. Even the sand takes on the appearance of granite in its terracing.

Seen from the base, this sand Mont Saint Michel reveals the breathtaking intricacy of its fine detailing.

Poised in mid-air, a massive portcullis carved from sand bars the front entrance. A masterpiece of sand engineering, it seems to have a physical integrity that sand simply does not have. Who — or what — lurks inside?

The towering spire of the Abbey pierced the oceanside sky at a height of 24 feet. The entire project was nearly 100 feet in circumference, and took the labor of 60 builders for four dawn-to-dusk days.

Saint Basil's Cathedral on Red Square is a worldwide symbol of Russian Orthodoxy. It is the home of the Patriarch of Moscow and was once the spiritual center of Holy Russia.

Almost unbelievably encrusted with history, Saint Basil's is the heartline of czarist power. Even the name means "holy emperor." It was to be the refuge of Orthodoxy after the mother church of the East, Saint Sophia ("holy wisdom") of Constantinople, fell to the Turks in 1453.

The Kremlin

The Kremlin was born in the outlandish nightmare of an early medieval Russian named Stephen Kuchka. He was hunting near the Moskva River with some friends when he witnessed a frightening and bizarre event.

A huge wild boar charged at the hunting party from a thicket they were approaching—roaring, head lowered, tusks glistening in the sun. Just as the hunters were scattering to run for their lives, an enormous winged creature appeared overhead, blotting out the sun's light.

The terrified hunters later swore that the gigantic bird had been an eagle with two heads. Whatever it was, it must have been a leviathan creature, for it scooped the boar up in its talons and soared straight up into the afternoon sky to a height where it was only a small dot in the blue. Then it dropped the boar, which crashed, mangled, down onto the top of a nearby hill.

That night the hunters made camp on the site of the boar's fall, and Stephen Kuchka had a prophetic dream. He saw a great city built on the site of the boar's demise: a great city centered upon an even greater fortress. The fortress had chalk-white battlements that ringed a thousand gold-domed churches; all the churches were ringing their bells. And while the bells were ringing, an

uncountable number of heads and decapitated bodies were flung from the walls of the white fortress into the nearby river. Stephen awoke from his dream in a sweat.

But he was not so frightened by the dream that he left the place. Indeed, he founded a city on the site and called it Kuchkovo. The center of his city was a wooden citadel later called the Kremlin.

The wooden city and fortress were destroyed in an inferno of blood and fire in the year 1238, when all of Eastern Europe succumbed to the swords of the Golden Horde, the Mongol barbarians of Genghis Khan. The invaders of Kuchkovo were under the lead of the Great Khan's nephew, Batu Khan, and they left not one inhabitant of the town

This fairy-land of onion-shaped domes and soaring towers is a twilight view of the Kremlin, perhaps the best-known single castle in the world. Born in the legend of Stephen Kuchka in the mists of semi-historical

tales, the Kremlin has been home to some of the arch-villains of all time. These halls resounded to the footsteps of Ivan the Terrible and Boris Godunov. It was also the power haven of Lenin and Stalin.

alive, nor one building standing. Everything was consumed by fire.

But Moscow and the Kremlin have a phoenix-like quality. More than once they have risen from the flames of conquest stronger, bigger, and more spectacular. And this first destruction was just such a case. The new city, named Moscow, that arose on the site was considerably grander than Kuchkovo had ever been.

The Kremlin has always been a focus of intrigue, foul play, and power. It was the site of the atrocities of Ivan the Terrible in the sixteenth century—and the unification of Russia by the same vengeful ruler. Legend has it that the Kremlin witnessed the murder of Ivan's infant heir, Dmitri, by the infamous Czar Boris Godunov. It

was certainly the home of Boris' descent into insanity as a false Dmitri swept into Russia from Poland, leveling all resistance with fire and sword.

It became, in fact, such a labyrinth of plots and counter-plots that Peter the Great decided to remove the government of Russia to another location. Just as the French monarchs had found it convenient to rule from Versailles instead of Paris, the czars after Peter ruled from Saint Petersburg instead of Moscow. By leaving the Kremlin to molder and decay, they left behind the murderous coups and intrigues of Moscow. And so

the Kremlin was virtually deserted for nearly 200 years, from the early eighteenth century until the early twentieth century.

But Lenin saw the value of the Kremlin, which had acquired an aura of overpowering Russian-ness and sanctity during its 200-year vacancy. The Bolshevik government placed itself squarely in the heart of Russia by locating itself in the Kremlin. And the intrigues began again as though they had never ceased. The death of Stalin is only one of a series of unresolved mysteries that the Kremlin holds the answer to and refuses to divulge.

The last wholesale destruction of Moscow and the Kremlin was at the climax of Napoleon's career in the year 1812. Napoleon had had

Looking for all the world like an enormous gingerbread house, the "real" Saint Basil's is a fantasy in color as well as in swirls of design. No two domes are the same; each is of stone or brick — although the feeling of waving flags is unavoidable.

dreams of cowering Russian nobles cringing at his feet and handing him the keys of the Kremlin. When he arrived in Moscow at the beginning of winter, he found not only the palace, but the entire city, totally deserted—and ablaze. The fleeing Muscovites had sacrificed their city rather than see it in the hands of an enemy invader. Their revenge was complete when Napoleon's *Grande Armée* was decimated by a combination of Russian guerrilla action and the devastating Russian winter. But the Kremlin and Moscow lay in ashes, under several meters of snow, behind them.

Once again it sprang back to life—with more gilt, more cupolas, and more Russian grandeur than ever before.

The Kremlin figures in much of Russia's history and promises to survive as a supreme crown of Russian achievement.

If the real Saint Basil's is a gingerbread house, this Saint Basil's of sand looks as if it came straight out of the oven — before icing.

The sand architects reproduced each dome absolutely faithfully — every swirl in place.

The 8-foot-high product of a single day's endeavors by four adult sandcastlers and two children as elfish assistants, Saint Basil's must have figured in the dreams of those youngsters for a long time.

Windsor Castle

Windsor has seen its moments of tragedy, of glory, and of unforgettable pageantry. It was founded in blood by William the Conqueror, who set up *motte-and-donjon* castles all over his new kingdom to subjugate the inhabitants. As the command headquarters of a brutal invading army, the Norman Tower (also called the Round Tower) was the first bit of Windsor to gaze out over the surrounding meadows and forests.

Soon after its founding, however, it began to grow. And it has continued to grow over the centuries until it is today one of the world's largest castles. Its proximity to London has made it a convenient hideaway for kings and queens, who traditionally made their strongest alliances with the people of London.

But there have been British monarchs for whom even Windsor could do very little. Such a one was the hapless King John. He was the youngest son of Henry II and Queen Eleanor of Aquitaine, but whereas his elder brothers were legendarily handsome—blond, muscular, tall—John was short, spindly, and ill-favored. And whereas his brother, Richard the Lion-Hearted, won the favor of the entire Christian world with his bravery and his personal magnetism, John managed to alienate virtually every noble in his entire kingdom.

John's regency during King Richard's absence at the Crusades had been an abomination on the land, one to this day remembered in the Robin Hood legends—the evil Sheriff of Nottingham and his wicked overlord, Prince John. But if his regency had been difficult to handle, his reign was impossible. In addition to his highhanded Plantagenet ways, he had been a loser in war.

During June 1215, King John knew that the barons of England had had enough. His entourage at Windsor grew smaller by the day, as more and more of his personal company went over to the baronial party. When his friends were down to seven—out of all the nobles in England—John decided to put a good face on it and give in. He got on his horse and rode to face the barons at a marshy meadow five miles east of Windsor. It was called Runnymede, and that day saw the first important capitulation of the British crown to democratic rights; that day John signed a document that ever since has been known as the Great Charter, the Magna Carta.

Years later, in the reign of Edward III, the Black Death hit England with such force that it may have killed upwards of half the population. Since it was thought at the time that the air in the cities was the carrier of the plague, the king moved himself and his party to the country for the duration of the plague. Windsor became the plague capital of the country.

Traditionally it has been said that it happened at a dance given by the king. One of the court ladies, during a high spin, lost one of her garters, which fell noticeably to the floor. Moral standards of the day declared a garter to be an unmentionable piece of clothing. But the king, every inch the courtly gentleman (and the ladies' man), retrieved the offending garter and handed it back to the lady who owned it. The eyebrows of the court rose in unison and the king stood up and declared, *"Honi soit qui mal y pense,"* or, "Evil is in the mind of the person who thinks evil." Shortly thereafter, Edward swore to make a lady's garter the most desirable piece of male attire in the world. To do that, he founded a knightly order: the Order of the Garter. Since this declaration had been made at Windsor, the new Chapel of St. George was proclaimed to be the Garter Chapel—as it has been known ever since.

Monarchs with a particular need for privacy have always felt at home at Windsor. Charles II, the profligate and charming king of the Restoration, spent a great deal of time there. He modernized the ancient castle by adding windows and a long gallery, apparently to put a little life into what must have been a rather gloomy old building. In Charles II's time, Windsor was already 600 years old.

One hundred and fifty years after Charles II died, England once again became a kingdom with a retiring monarch. This time it was George III, the king who lost America. George was an extremely moral man, unlike Charles II, but he had a problem which required absolute privacy: He was going mad. He wandered through the parks of Windsor talking to the trees; he raged at trivia; he cried copiously; he never recovered.

George IV was a monarch who would leave his mark on England architecturally. He built the edifice we know today as Buckingham Palace, although he never lived in

Rising from the riverside in all its Gothic Revival splendor, Windsor — seat of kings and queens for nearly a thousand years — displays more turrets than the eye can count. The Round Tower was built by William the Conqueror during the Conquest, but the tower in this picture was heightened and enhanced by Jeffry Wyatt during the reign of George IV (1820-1830).

it. But Windsor Castle was George IV's pride and remains his monument.

Windsor had endured nearly eight centuries of royal whim and neglect when George IV decided to fix it up a bit. George hired a visionary architect, Jeffry Wyatt, to redo the castle—which Wyatt did, to the tune of over a million pounds. As a result of Wyatt's renovation, Windsor has features that were considered absurdly useless at the time. Its great front gate, for instance, has a *fake* port-cullis slot above it, one that was added by Wyatt to *simulate* the feeling of what he considered to be an accurate medieval style. The corner masonry is simulated likewise; artificial mortar joints decorate the freestone blocks of its walls.

Queen Victoria

But Wyatt, laughed at though he was at the time, created a worldwide fashion by his rebuilding of Windsor. It was called the "Gothic Revival," and it is to Wyatt, therefore, that we owe the Houses of Parliament and much that is most fanciful in Victorian architecture.

The delicate, nearly Oriental, splendor of St. George's Chapel at Windsor is the architectural bequest of Edward III, one of the great Plantagenet kings of England.

During a sojourn at Windsor while the Black Death was raging in London, Edward III founded the Order of the Knights of the Garter, patterned directly on the legends of King Arthur's Round Table. The Garter has been the most coveted chivalric order in the world for over 600 years.

This Windsor replica is the product of 1600 hours of work by 40 sand crafters. It covered 6600 square feet of beach and rose 26 feet from the tideline.

Accurate to the last detail, this royal sandcastle includes an interpretation of the medieval Windsor village surrounding the castle.

Like medieval craftsmen at work, two sandcastlers huddle over the detailing of Charles IV's jewel-like castle, Karlštejn.

High on a crag in the Bohemian forest, Karlštejn was built by the late medieval emperor as a palace of peace and meditative splendor. Its richly detailed interiors were encrusted with gold leaf and jewels, as befitted the home of a regal descendant of Charlemagne.

Karlštejn

Prague, the capital of modern Czechoslovakia, was once the capital of the Kingdom of Bohemia, a monarchy of an eccentric style. First of all, though the monarch was called a *king,* he was himself a subject of the Holy Roman Emperor. Second, like several Eastern European monarchies, the throne of Bohemia was an elective position.

It was during the time of emperors and kings that Prague earned its nickname, "City of a Hundred Spires." It is a perfect city to look at: the Voltava River ambles through the center of town, giving ample opportunity to generations of builders of graceful bridges, riverfront homes and public buildings, sidewalk cafes, and towering churches. The "hundred spires" of the city's name are the Gothic steeples of more than a hundred superb churches.

But Prague, as picturesque and cosmopolitan as it may have been in its heyday, was not a place of solitude for a man of international affairs. Such a man was the Holy Roman Emperor, Charles IV (1348-1355), the last member of the House of Luxembourg to occupy the throne of Charlemagne, to wear the ancient crown of the father of Western civilization.

As Holy Roman Emperor, Charles's capital was any of a number of imperial cities: Brussels, Vienna, Salzburg. But Charles had a fondness for Bohemia (he was also the elective King of Bohemia), and it was in the lush forests of southwest Bohemia that he chose to build the magnificent retreat that came to be called, after him, Karlštejn (Charles's Castle).

The nearby Berounka river wanders through primeval forest, chasing through gorges, with a waterfall here and there. And suddenly, high above, looms a formidable sight: It is Karlštejn. Like a castle out of a fairy story, it totally dominates the horizon for miles in every direction.

This is Kafka territory. His masterwork, *The Castle,* might have been set in the nondescript Bohemian village at the base of the castle's glacis. It is also the countryside that Karel Capek had in mind when he created the phantasmagoric nightmare of *The Makropoulos Affair,* in which an elixir of eternal youth is developed for the Emperor Rudolf II, then tested on an unwitting girl who is doomed to live nearly 350 years as a result. Rudolf II was a longtime tenant of Karlštejn.

But it was Charles IV who built Karlštejn, and he built it as an ideal home for the ideal medieval monarch. It is a self-contained world; one of the most remarkable things about the castle today is the completeness with which it approached life.

There is a knights' hall and a

Basking in the late-afternoon summer sun, this Karlštejn of sand hardly seems the locale of one of the central events of the early Reformation. It was in Karlštejn that the followers of Jan Huss took refuge when that unfortunate heretic was condemned by the church courts.

The sun's rays cast a friendlier aspect on Karlštejn, giving it the peaceful glow its builder intended 600 years ago.

knights' chapel. There is a banqueting hall, and cavernous kitchens to supply food. There are royal apartments and semi-royal apartments and barracks. No aspect of courtly life is left unattended. For the king-emperor's private worship, there was a chapel for music and a chapel for contemplation.

And the art that is built into the castle is astounding. The largest chapel is built in the shape of a cruciform; it is sumptuous almost beyond belief: A radiant gilded ceiling contains, in oil, an exact replica of the nighttime sky—with all the stars and the moon in place as on the vernal equinox. The walls of the same chapel are adorned with mosaics made entirely out of semi-precious stones. The remaining space is covered with vignettes of life painted by Theoderich.

The bedroom built for Charles IV was enough to make even an emperor sigh. It is crusted with jewels and gold, with damask silk from the Levant, with furniture made by the finest craftsmen of Europe, and with—local splendor —the most exquisite Bohemian glass to be seen anywhere. It was this bedroom that Charles built as a repository for the crown jewels of the empire.

But shortly after Charles's death, the repose of emperors became a fortress in earnest. The visionary religious leader, Jan Huss, the forerunner of the Reformation, rose like a firebrand in Bohemia during the reign of King Wenceslaus IV. The Hussite partisans battled against the Catholic forces in one of the first pitched civil wars in European history. The tragic end for Huss himself was the heretic's martyr-dom—he was burned at the stake in the year 1415. But ever afterwards, Bohemia was a country

wracked by religious dissent.

The grim passage of the Thirty Years War in the seventeenth century left Bohemia a land of invasion and re-invasion: one year in the hands of the Protestant Frederick (the "Winter King"), the next year held in the iron gauntlet of the vengeful Emperor Ferdinand, an orthodox Catholic.

And Karlštejn was never again, after Huss, the peaceful country villa it was meant to be. It became for a time a dower property of the Queens of Bohemia, and so probably echoed with frivolous laughter from time to time. But only with Charles IV and Rudolf II was it a seat of empire.

Today Karlštejn is a powerful symbol of Bohemian (and Czech) liberty. It remains a statement of the dream of a powerful medieval emperor: a sylvan retreat resplendent with the trappings of majesty, the opulence that only empire could justify. Few people— few emperors—have left behind monuments of such surpassing beauty.

Visualized here as it must have been in the times before the two world wars, Karlštejn looks the picture of serenity: the perfect country palace.

In reality, it was the location of considerable intrigue and international political maneuvering. It was in these walls that one Doktor Makropoulos (according to Bohemian author, Karel Capek) developed an elixir of eternal life for Rudolf II. The alchemist doctor tested the life-preserving liquid on his own daughter, Elena, who was doomed to an abysmally unhappy 350-year life as a result.

After being the principal court of emperors Charles IV and Rudolf II, Karlštejn was given to the Queens of Bohemia as a retreat from the rigors of court life in Prague.

It was for years the repository of the crown jewels of Bohemia, because it commanded a perfect defense from all angles. The steep curtain wall was surely a discouraging sight to would-be thieves.

This jewel-like replica on a sandy beach in Southern California was small — barely 4 feet tall — but would-be princesses and real Bohemians crowded the building site in silent awe that would have satisfied the mightiest Emperor.

The Marksburg

In lonely splendor the Marksburg perches above the village of Braubach-am-Rhein, the last remaining memento of an age when the robber barons of the Rhine controlled a river that was second only to the Tiber in historical importance. All the other Rhinecastles have fallen into ruins; only the Marksburg survives intact.

Not far down the river is the rock of the infamous Lorelei, that golden siren of German legend who lured men to a watery grave with the sound of her beautiful voice. She sat on the top of the Lorelei Rock all night long, combing her golden hair; and as she combed she sang, and none could withstand the witchery of her song.

Her father was the Rhine itself, and she lived underwater by day; it was by night that she cast her deadly spells. Her suitors found their bleary ends in her Crystal Palace beneath the same waters that flow by the Marksburg today.

The waters of this same Rhine hid the wonders of the elfin race of the Nibelung, who forged a golden ring that bestowed all power and riches on its owners. The saga of the Ring of the Nibelung became one of the great theatrical masterpieces of all time, when Richard Wagner created his great Ring Cycle to tell the story: "The Rhine Gold," "The Valkyries," "Siegfried," and "The Twilight of the Gods."

Wagner told, in another story, of a medieval minstrel named Walter von der Vogelweide, one of the unsuccessful suitors of the lovely Elisabeth in "Tannhauser." It was this same Walter who wrote the saga of the Counts of Katzenellenbogen, who built the Marksburg. But these Germanic warlords were not the first settlers of the place.

Caius Drusus, called "Germanicus," led a Roman army through this place in the first decade before the birth of Christ.

Excavations have discovered ruins of a Roman town beneath the current Braubach; these ruins may be the town founded by Drusus—the same Drusus who was later poisoned by his own son, the future Emperor Caligula, one of the maddest and cruelest monarchs in the history of the world.

The medieval town and citadel were nearly destroyed by a great fire in 1613, during the early skirmishes of the Thirty Years War. It had a dark reputation for hundreds of years before and after that bloody war.

Built as a fortress for a lawless, marauding family whose defenseless prey were the boats on the mighty Rhine, the Marksburg saw long duty as a state prison. It was said to have the most gruesomely well-equipped torture chamber in Europe. The screams of the dying and the soon-to-die must have echoed through the bleak stone corridors with ferocious regularity.

The Marksburg was named for the Markus Tower, dedicated to Saint Mark the Evangelist, which was finished by one of the early Counts of Katzenellenbogen, Philip I, in 1437. Opposite on the

Today's Marksburg is the last Rhine castle left to us. All the others are in ruins. It was given to posterity by Kaiser Wilhelm II, and is today the headquarters in Germany of the International Castles-Institute.

The tallest of the castle's towers, the Markus Tower was named for Saint Mark the Evangelist. In its time, the Marksburg held, beneath Saint Mark's Tower, one of the most fearsome torture chambers in all Europe.

river is Rhense, dating from 1370, built by command of the Emperor Charles IV as the site of Imperial Diets and Electoral Assemblies. An outlandish throne was carved out of living rock at Rhense, surmounting a dais approached by eighteen steps—giving the Holy Roman Emperor some of the Asian dignity of the fabled emperors of Constantinople.

It was said of Rhense that when the emperor's trumpets blew there, all four of the Imperial Electors could hear it in their castles: the Elector of Mayence at Lahneck, the Archbishop of Treves at Stolzenfels, the Archbishop of Cologne at Rhense, and the Electoral Count of the Palatinate at his fortress of the Marksburg.

The Marksburg has had many owners. The builders lost possession of it as an outcome of the Thirty Years' War, when it passed to the state of Hesse-Darmstadt in 1651. Then as an aftermath of the Napoleonic Wars, it was appropriated by the government of Nassau as a state prison. The German Empire under Kaiser Wilhelm II took possession of it in the late nineteenth century.

The warlike kaiser was an emperor of artistic discernment, especially when it came to German artifacts and architecture. It was the kaiser who founded the Society for the Preservation of German Castles—and he who gave the Marksburg to the Society as a museum.

The Marksburg has been completely restored, and today is resplendent with what might well have been its original furnishings. A magnificent collection of armor greets today's visitor, along with centuries of hand-held weapons. But perhaps most fascinating, because the restoration of the castle has been so lovingly carried out, one can glimpse the lifestyle of an age long gone.

Stews seem to simmer on the hearths in great iron pots. One can sense the activity of cooks, scullery maids, servers, butlers, and pages in the well-appointed medieval kitchen. And on at least three sides of the castle, the view has

not changed appreciably in several hundred years. Still the sweet grapes of the Rhine grow on the hillsides. Still the castle commands a landlocked peninsula created by the great Rhine and two minor tributaries, the Grosse and the Zolbach. And still the Braubacher Wald, the dense Bavarian forest, takes the horizon back to pre-history.

At least three Holy Roman Emperors lodged here; Counts Palatine by the score were landlords. Once there were castles on the Rhine almost more than a person could count. Today only the Marksburg survives.

But it is a paragon of Rhineland architecture, and a perfect dream castle. Surmounting an enormous, solid rock, it could never have been sapped or mined, because its foundations were granite. Higher than any land for miles, it could never have been taken by surprise.

Today's Marksburg is still surrounded by the medieval curtain wall easily visible in old drawings and woodcuts. But it is much overgrown with the verdant brush and greenery that are native to the region. The Marksburg is the headquarters of the Internationales Burgen-Institut in Germany.

Voluptuous and deadly, the legendary Lorelei played her plaintive lament nightly in the mythology of the Rhine. With her beauty and her song she lured sailors to a watery, bloody death beneath the river, where she devoured them.

Situated on the shore of the Pacific Ocean, this Marksburg replica soared to a height of 8 feet at the top of the Markus Tower. The ghostly isolation of this sandcastle evokes tales of the Valhalla, Germany's answer to a warrior's heaven.

Bran Castle

Most of the castles we see in our dreams are patterned after what could be called the Norman model. They have round towers capped with flying pennants; they have crenelated curtain walls and half-timbered courtyard buildings. Most of all, they are inhabited by golden knights in Ivanhoe chain mail—and by damsels with tall, pointed hats and damask gowns. The picture is altogether a Western European one and could have been played anywhere from Scotland to Spain over a period of 300 years.

But there is another type of castle that lurks in the sub-conscious, ready to spring out in nights of restless sleep. It is a bleak and forbidding mountain fastness—more like an eagle's nest than a home for human beings. It blends into the craggy and barren peaks of black mountains in Transylvania or Carpathia. And it is inhabited by vampires.

The archetype of the vampire's castle is Bran Castle near Poiana Brasov in Romania. Built in the late fifteenth century, it was the stronghold of Vlad Dracul, a Wallachian nobleman and patriot. It is from this Vlad that the legend of Nosferatu was given birth. Bram Stoker's classic novel flashed

the name of this relatively obscure Eastern European across the world as Dracula: Count Dracula.

Vlad Dracul lived in a bloody era. Most of modern Romania was at one time or another connected with the old Byzantine Roman Empire, which had its capital at Constantinople. By the dawn of the fifteenth century, the godlike emperors of the White City of the Bosporus, as the capital was called, had been losing ground for centuries. The advance of Islam was to prove finally unstoppable, and the holy city of Constantin-ople fell to the scimitars of Maomet II. The last emperor in a line that stretched back to Julius Caesar was slaughtered in his palace; his name was John Paleologus.

The fall of Constantinople in 1453 put Wallachia (a section of what is today Romania) in a fairly precarious position. While Constantinople had not been able for years to provide any meaningful defense against invasion, its

reputation as the Queen of the East had held together a series of states along the Black Sea with a sort of psychological glue. And now everything fell apart. Vlad Dracul was the man of the hour.

He was also fiendishly cruel. His historical nickname was Vlad the Impaler, from a preference of his for a particularly gruesome mode of execution of enemies captured in battle. It was said of him that he would dine as he watched the writhing bodies of his enemies rammed onto sharp wooden stakes.

To give the real Vlad his due, he was not much different in his brutal acts from other leaders of his day. But the norm at that time was a bit more than most political leaders of today would consider advisable.

But Vlad was a Slav and a Wallachian patriot, and he did not tolerate foreigners well. While most of his victims were Turks and southern invaders, he did turn his bloodthirsty attentions against people from what would be today Poland and Germany. It is to these victims of his rage that we owe the vampire legend: the fiend suckled on blood, with the strength of a hundred strong men in each arm.

The vampire legend owes much to the career of Vlad Dracul. His

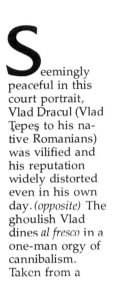Seemingly peaceful in this court portrait, Vlad Dracul (Vlad Țepeș to his native Romanians) was vilified and his reputation widely distorted even in his own day. *(opposite)* The ghoulish Vlad dines *al fresco* in a one-man orgy of cannibalism. Taken from a political pamphlet printed in Strasbourg in 1500, the Vlad shown here is grossly exaggerated from the real Vlad Țepeș.

But mistreated as he has been by history and literature, Vlad was a warrior of particularly gruesome tactics.

Bran Castle forms the backdrop for his grisly feast.

custom (his delight, as it was said) of impaling gave us the method by which a vampire must be killed—with a wooden stake through the heart. His ferocious defense of his country gave us the need for a vampire to rest on his native soil during his times of sleep. And his general reputation gave the story that he drank blood.

His method of torture was well documented, although it is a matter of conjecture how accurate the reports were. "Stakes piercing their head, their breast, their buttocks and the middle of their entrails, with the stake emerging from their mouths." It would be enough to start a rumor of vampirism.

And there is no doubt, no doubt whatsoever, that Bran Castle is the castle of Vlad. It was built just before his sudden death in 1476. It was said at the time that his head was sent to the Sultan as a present. But some bones were found in a nearby monastery a few years ago that were tentatively identified as his. And the suspicion has never been defeated that he roams his country still, his repulsive longing for gore forever unsated. As the visitor to Bran looks up at the castle against a full moon, it could well be a huge monster bat, its towers like claws or fangs, clinging to its rocky precipice like a creature from a horrible nightmare.

33

Today's Bran Castle belies its bloody and magnificent history. Peaceful and serene in the clear Wallachian sunshine, it is one of the chief tourist attractions of modern Romania.

Until the late Middle Ages, the Black Sea countries were part of the protective alliance centered on Constantinople — the Byzantine Empire. But Constantinople fell in 1453 to the Turks, and areas like Wallachia were left to fend for themselves. Patriots like Vlad Țepeș held the line against the Infidel, sometimes against

nearly incredible odds. The ferocity of Vlad's retaliation against his enemies was a reaction to the viciousness of war.

It is said that, when he died in battle, Vlad's head was sent in a barrel of vinegar to the Sultan as proof that he was dead at last.

But Vlad was sighted again and again haunting the mountain recesses of his home, giving birth to the legend of his immortality. Bran even today seems perched, ready to fly off into the night like a gigantic vampire bat under the full moon.

Transported magically to a mist-enshrouded seashore, this Bran replica is much closer to the feeling of Dracula than even the original in Romania. It recalls the landing of the count in England, his bloody mist seeping through the cobweb-hung halls of the deserted Colfax castle.

In Bram Stoker's classic novel, *Dracula,* the vampire lord came ashore from a ghost ship that drifted into an English harbor. When it found land, a fire-eyed hound leapt ashore (Dracula in one of his many forms), and disappeared into the fog.

This sand version of Bran Castle was a modest 6 feet tall, but its inhabitants live forever in nightmares worldwide.

3

The Parts of Castles

Castles did not originate in a single geographic location; early civilizations around the world knew the need for defense as soon as they began to recognize the inevitable fact that not all societies are friendly to each other.

The world's oldest societies all built castles and fortified cities, because the history of mankind is a history of struggle. Castles began to be built a long time before history was first recorded.

But no structure built by man is immortal, and few of these early citadels are still with us. Such survivors as there are, are mere hints of former strength and glory. Today's visitor to the ruins of mighty Troy may feel a certain awe in treading the same soil that Hector and Achilles fought on, but it is primarily in the imagination that Troy continues to exist. The

site is more a series of trenches and partially finished excavations than a city these days. The same is true of Agamemnon's fortress city of Mycenae in southern Greece. The same is true of Nineveh, of Thebes, of Chichen Itza.

Some castle sites from the far reaches of ancient history hold particular fascination. Such a site is Maiden Castle on the southern coast of England, facing the whitecaps and breakers of the English Channel and longing for a brief view of Brittany across the water.

Maiden Castle today is merely

a series of gargantuan earthen circles, all of them grown over with the lush greenery of ages. But it must have been a splendid castle long ago. It was built by a vanished race of people historians know only as Iberians. They may have entered the British Isles across a now-vanished land bridge from Calais to Dover, or they may have navigated the Channel in small boats. But however they settled the islands, they were already long gone when the first accounts of England were recorded by Julius Caesar.

By the time Caesar crossed the

A surviv- or of the mists of prehistory, Maiden Castle in Dorset, England, was built by a race of people who had van- ished even before the Celts took over Britain.

The concentric rings of earth that comprise the re- mains of this titanic fortifica- tion bear the marks of millenia of erosion, re- markably like a sandcastle eaten away by the tide.

This is Thomas Hardy country, and it was a ruin such as this that marked the fatal meeting of hus- band and lost wife in *The Mayor of Casterbridge*.

Channel, the Iberians had been driven out of the fertile valleys of England and were probably hidden in refuge in the black mountains of Wales, or in the rocky landscapes of Cornwall. They had been vanquished by invaders whom we know as Celts.

Maiden Castle was probably very much as it is today when armored Romans first saw it over 2,000 years ago. It is of the vintage of Stonehenge, and it is just as mysterious. The heroic people who built it and the brilliant architect(s) who planned it, who staked out the perfectly concentric fortifications, will never emerge from the mists of time. We can only guess at who they were.

Oddly, today's Maiden Castle is an object lesson for the sand- castler. Looking at it from the air, it looks like a a marvelous sandcastle partially leveled by the tide. It has that rounded look that nature produces by slow erosion. It looks as though it were ready to blend back into the ground it sprang from without a trace.

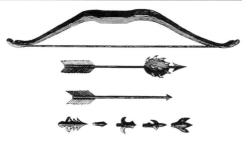

What Is a Castle?

In the broadest sense, a castle is any fortification against invasion or attack. But the castles we build on the beaches of the world are more precisely fortified residences.

Camelot, for instance, was principally the residence of King

Arthur and his court. It was defended by the storied Knights of the Round Table, but it was made defensible by the most massive ramparts in the world, according to the legend.

When the word "castle" is used, today's sandcastler is likely to picture a Norman castle, although the styles and floorplans of castles around the world are as varied as the peoples who built them. The Norman castle became, over four or five centuries, the predominant style throughout Europe and the Middle East, and it became the locus of most European legends and fairy tales. Spain's El Cid is usually pictured in a Norman castle, as is England's Richard the Lion-Hearted, France's Charlemagne, and the rest of the white knights of song and history.

The Norman Castle

The Normans were originally Vikings; they swept across what is today northern France in the eighth and ninth centuries. They

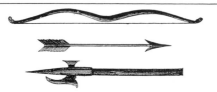

were a striking race: tall, fair, even-featured. And they were warriors.

They overran northern France (Gaul), and dispossessed the native inhabitants there, claiming it for their own. The area became known as the Land of the Norsemen—Normandy.

But they never lost their Viking spirit, their longing for travel, adventure, and conquest. During the expanse of time we know as the Middle Ages, the Normans became overlords of lands as far-flung as England, Sicily, and Jerusalem—as well as their home fiefdom of Normandy. They became some of the most cosmopolitan people of their time. And they were the originators of much of the remarkable art and architecture of their time. It is to the Normans that we owe the Gothic cathedrals of Chartres, Rouen, and Amiens—as well as the Gothic minsters of England: Westminster Abbey, York Minster, and Salisbury Cathedral. The Normans invented stained glass and took it to its greatest glory in the twelfth and thirteenth centuries.

More important to the subject of this book, however, it was the Norman-designed castle that became the textbook for castle builders throughout the Middle Ages. They were without doubt the preeminent warriors of their day, and it was the Normans who led the European pack in fortification, war machines, siege technique, and weaponry.

The Motte

There were fortified places all over Europe before the Normans

arrived. England, for instance, was dotted with Anglo-Saxon and Danish stockades prior to the invasion, in 1066, by William the Conqueror, Duke of Normandy. But there was a dramatic change in fortification style immediately after the conquest.

The Normans had evolved a method of building that was as predictable and as efficient as the wars they waged. It was probably learned from rebuilding over the smoking ruins of their conquered foes. The essence of their fortification style was a *motte.*

A motte is an artificial hill, invented by the Normans for tactical advantage. The old adage that height has the upper hand was put to practical use by the innovation of the motte. Now Normans did not have to look for a location on high ground; they created the high ground themselves.

Mottes were created by digging circular, or nearly circular, trenches and simply throwing the earth inward—very much like the way a modern sandcastler would pile up dirt in an artificial mountain to build on. But of course Norman mottes were considerably larger than most sandcastles.

The foundation of the motte was not entirely earthen; it usually contained all manner of rubble. Mottes were frequently built on the sites of conquered villages or towns. The building materials made admirable underpinnings

for the new motte. Excavations under existing mottes have yielded ample proof of the character of Norman landfill.

The Motte would be surmounted by a wooden stockade, at first, surrounded by pointed stakes. But soon after would follow the donjon—the first stage of the great Norman castle.

The Donjon or Keep

The Norman was not a conqueror to trust his safety to a mere wooden palisade. His own history would have proved to him that anything wooden was vulnerable to attack by fire. A dozen archers with fire-tipped arrows could destroy a timber fortification in short order during a concerted battle.

What was needed was something that would withstand even the siege of a horde of warriors—and that something would have to be made of stone. The Norman solution was a thick-walled tower called a *donjon.*

It was a bleak-looking and bleak-living structure in the beginning, but it was the answer to a warlord's prayers. It was constructed in a variety of shapes—square, round, elliptical—but whatever the architectural niceties about it, it was all but impregnable to attack.

With walls up to thirty feet thick, it stood atop the motte like a stone sentinel, guarding all the land within sight. Because it commanded such height, it became both a citadel and a symbol of power. It could be seen from great distances and it was in many cases the only stone building for many leagues in any

The year 1066 brought the Norman Conquest to the island of Britain, and with it came a new style of fortification.

Whereas Anglo-Saxon "castles" had been largely stockades much

like U.S. Cavalry forts, the Norman warlords built in stone. Cliffords Tower is the core building of the castle of York. The famous "White Tower" *(below)* was the palatial home of William the Bastard, the "Kinges Tour offe London."

direction. It is from the donjon that modern phrases such as "a tower of power" and "a tour de force" come.

And it is also the source of another, a more ominous, word— a word that represents the grim side of power. For as the donjon was a tool and a symbol of oppression, it became a prison and a place of execution. It became a *dungeon.* The word donjon is medieval French for "the lord's home." It is, in fact, the same root word as the modern *dominion,* but without the middle syllable.

The donjon was built in a hurry, and it appeared in a variety of building styles. The most polished donjons were made of a material called *ashlar,* a smoothly cut and finished stone construction. Most donjons were, however, made of rubble dumped between parallel walls, in a manner very similar to modern sandcastle construction. Walls erected by this "sandwich" method were sometimes enormously thick— up to twelve feet. And they had a practical aspect as well, because if someone tried to undermine them, they caved in from the middle, sending tons of

rocky rubble down onto the sappers.

This stark tower remained the core of the Norman castle for a hundred years, until one of the great events of the Middle Ages set Europe ablaze with passion. That event was the First Crusade.

Constantinople:
The Queen of the East

The Roman Empire in the West had fallen in 476 AD, succumbing to the barbarian tribes that had overrun Italy repeatedly for over a century. Despite attempts to revive old Roman imperial rule, it was never again a seat of empire.

But the Roman Empire in the East was an entirely different matter. The Emperor Diocletian had decided that the empire was too widespread to administer from a single imperial capital and thus had split the empire into two distinct halves. The Eastern Empire was administered from an entirely new city built at the mouth of the Black Sea: Constantinople, so called for the Emperor Constantine who built it. The Eastern capital, the "New Rome," was built on what was

then thought to be the site of ancient Troy (mistakenly, as it turned out). And it held out for a thousand years after Rome fell.

All the wisdom and sophistication of Greece, Persia, and Rome was preserved at Constantinople. It was a city of overwhelming beauty, wealth, and modernity. Its citizens were using running water when the citizens of Norman donjons were sitting around smoky fires in one-room towers. Constantinople was a dazzling and storied survivor. Its emperor was a remote and autocratic ruler who was treated much like a god—or like a later emperor of China—although Constantinople was solidly Christian and did not believe its emperors to be divine.

Constantinople lay directly in the path of the Crusades, as the crude vulgarians of Western Europe flocked to the Holy Land to free the Holy places from the Infidel. The emperors of Constantinople were wary of these heavily armed and vicious Europeans, and were happy to give them provisions and see them depart for their battles in

41

modern-day Syria, Lebanon, and Israel. But the soldiers carried back to Europe, when they finally returned, dreams of splendor and tales of Constantinople's glory—and her walls.

The Castle Expands

Soon after the First Crusade, the simple donjon of the Norman warlord began to see real expansion. There was no way to convince the noblemen of the Crusades that they ought to continue to live in what they could now see was little better than a hovel, after seeing the mind-boggling wealth and beauty of Constantinople.

The practical addition to the average castle was the first *curtain wall.* Now the lord not only had his motte and donjon, he also had a miniature walled city as his home, which became known as a *manor* or *manoir.* The yard created by the addition of curtain walls was known as a *bailey* or *bailiwick,* and the lord's representative who oversaw the manor was the lord's *bailiff.*

With extensive walls to maintain and defend, such as those at Warwick Castle or Richmond Castle in England, or at Carcassonne in France, it became necessary to man them with regularly stationed corps of guards who could keep permanent watch over the countryside. The result

was the *castle walk,* or *parapet*—a kind of sidewalk along the tops of the walls.

Castle walks were defended by a device that, in our day, has become the hallmark of the medieval castle. That device was a system of *crenelations.* The castle defenders thought of crenelations as a series of gaps in an otherwise solid wall, but they were in reality just the opposite: a series of unreinforced walls unconnected to each other. Because of that, they were never very sturdy, and few crenelated walls survive intact today. At the time, nevertheless, they provided alternately a shield and shooting opportunity for parapet archers and warriors. The high section of the wall was a *merlon,* from the Italian for ravens, which perched on the walls waiting for carrion during battles. The lower sections of the walls were called *embrasures* or *crenels.*

Defenders of curtain walls, like defenders of donjons, would stop at no barbarity in warding off

enemies. Infantry who tried to scale walls were apt to have heavy boulders dropped on them from crenels—or huge vats of boiling water or superheated animal fat poured on them. After the Crusades brought back the ferocity of the Middle East, "Greek Fire" became a popular defender's device; it was like napalm and clung to a victim while it burned him to death. It had been originated by the scientists of Constantinople as a weapon to use at sea—to destroy enemy ships—because it continued to burn even while floating on water. It was a product of naturally appearing petroleum products, such as bitumen.

It was the appearance of the curtain wall after the Crusades that enabled the medieval castle to become, in many instances, centers of culture, commerce, and political intrigue. No longer were inhabitants restricted to the smoky, gigantic recesses of the primitive donjon.

In fact, with the discovery in the twelfth or thirteenth century of the chimney flue, private chambers became possible. It was, according to many modern experts, the development of the chimney flue that eventually led society to the upheavals of the eighteenth century: the French Revolution, the American Revolution, and the Seven Years' War. How? By

The central event of the Middle Ages was the series of holy wars that history has named the Crusades. Ostensibly fought to make the Holy Land safe for pilgrimage, the seven great crusades were actually waged for a variety of less savory reasons. But whatever their motivations, they were the soul of pageantry and chivalry. Between the Crusades and chivalric tournaments, the Middle Ages made an art form of the procession. And the sophistication of Constantinople (*opposite page*) was the primary cause of a new-found civility across Western Europe.

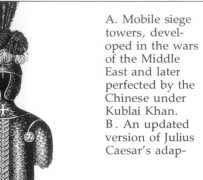

Warfare in the Age of Castles was a brutal affair, but one that developed a specialized technology that is fascinating in its own right.

Often thirst and starvation were the winners in a protracted siege, but the siege methods depicted here were employed with savage regularity:

A. Mobile siege towers, developed in the wars of the Middle East and later perfected by the Chinese under Kublai Khan.
B. An updated version of Julius Caesar's adaptation of Alexander the Great's shielded phalanx, concealing the murderous arrows of archers.
C. The suspended battering ram, pounding its way through yards of solid stone wall.

A

B

C

E arly medieval armor was designed to be practical in real warfare. It consisted largely of chain mail and thick leather tunics, although metal breastplates were common.

But as the nobility began to relegate warfare more and more to mercenaries, their armor became more and more ceremonial. The fully armored knight of the period of the Wars of the Roses in England (1400-1485) might have worn a hundred pounds of armor.

The fine craft of armory from the later Middle Ages and the early Renaissance is well illustrated here: finger-jointed gauntlets, plumed helmets, full horse armor.

Such suits of armor were frequent gifts among sovereigns. Henry VIII received a magnificent armor from the Emperor Maximilian; he in turn gave a suit of golden armor to Francis I, the French king whom he met at the Field of the Cloth of Gold.

Cinderella's Castle is probably the most widely dreamt-of fairy-tale residence in the world. And Cinderella herself appears in virtually every folk tradition.

Swept away from the drudgery of her life by the chimney, the beautiful, fragile young Cinderella becomes a princess in a castle that floats in a cloud of luxury and romance.

The Brothers Grimm, in 1826, wrote of Cinderella as "Aschenputel," although she has now become, to modern Germans, Aschenbrödel. She might have found her home in the magnificent fantasy of a demented Bavarian king, Ludwig II: Neuschwannstein.

The large castle shown here is a fantasy that came to life in Carlsbad, California, in 1980, as part of a flower festival. But it is a perfect palace for a magical girl like "La Gata Cenerentola" ("The Hearth Cat") from the 1634 Italian *Pentamerone*, Cinderella's earliest printed appearance.

This large fantastical, magical castle was the springtime dream of sandcastlers in Cardiff-by-the-Sea, California. But it is in just such a soaring edifice that Andrew Lang's heroine (yet another Cinderella), "Rashin Coatie," might have lived. Rashin Coatie was a legend in the Earl of Moray's Scottish domain in the nineteenth century.

The sandcastle at left was heroic in proportion: 18 feet tall. The castle on this page was a modest (in comparison) 12 feet tall.

The civilized splendor of Windsor — gilded, embellished, regal — is a real-life fairytale home for "Cendrillon," the Charles Perrault heroine, from whom we get our modern Cinderella.

Rapunzel! Rapunzel! Let down your long hair!''

We know for a fact (or a fantasy) that the fairytale favorite, Rapunzel, was held prisoner by a wicked witch in a tower — from which she was at length rescued by a braid-climbing cavalier.

If a real Rapunzel ever existed, what an enormous number of different types of castle tower might have been her house of confinement! Even in Western Europe, the styles over the centuries and across lands have been incredibly diverse.

The square keep could be a Norman stronghold; there is a Norman donjon of similar shape at Oxford. Then Rapunzel's prison would probably have been the small turret that surmounts the tower. The pennant-topped tower is a segment of the real Warwick Castle in England — the stronghold of the Marcher Earls who more than once disrupted the kingly succession in England.

The tower with

a conical roof is a type found commonly in southern France. The flight of stairs is a sandcastler's fantasy that would have made the real tower too easily vulnerable to invasion.

The round-topped tower is a type found commonly in Bavaria and southern Germany, and is a first cousin to one on the castle of Heidelberg. The elegant hexagonal tower is one of the remains of the ruined Ragland Castle on the border of England and Wales, pulled down by Cromwell because its defenses held too well in the Parliamentary Wars of 1642-1649.

The last tower was probably adapted by a well-educated sandcastler from a style prominent in northern Germany, in the cities of the Hanseatic League.

allowing a lord to live separate from his vassals.

Donjon life had mixed everyone together in the donjon's "great hall." Lord and lady, cook, pages, grooms—even prisoners held for ransom—all ate and slept together. The chimney enabled castle architects to build separate heated quarters for all. The chimney was thus eventually responsible for the vast gap that developed between rich and poor, the gap that was bridged by the terrors of Robespierre and Madame la Guillotine in 1793. The development of the chimney flue, together with the importation of the curtain wall, made the great castles of England and Europe the safest and the most comfortable places to live in the then known world.

The first areas built up inside the new curtain walls were attached to the walls themselves, where groups of soldiers would erect three-walled buildings as living quarters (the fourth wall being the curtain wall itself). These buildings were, in all likelihood, very similar to the surviving inside gatehouse at Caldicot Castle in England.

Although the normal vision of a castle in a fairy tale probably has a regular, even symmetrical, plan, most castles were wandering, asymmetrical affairs that suited themselves as closely as possible to the terrain. The castle of the Sires de Couci in northern France—reputedly the largest castle in the world in its heyday—was fitted most perfectly to its three-sided hilltop and remained

impregnable for 600 years on account of it. The magnificent ruin of Richard the Lion-Hearted's Château Gaillard needs no explanation when it comes to adaptation to the environment; it is nearly impossible to tell where the granite cliff leaves off and the castle begins.

Castles were built in all sizes and shapes. Towers could be round (as Clifford's Tower in York Castle), elliptical (as the Norman Keep at Windsor Castle), square (as in the Black Castle in Kilkenny, Ireland), stepped (as at Oxford), or any of a vast number of slightly irregular shapes.

The critical strength or damning weakness of any castle was its entrance. During the great age of castles, gunpowder had not yet been used with enough expertise or impact to breach castle walls (movies notwithstanding). Given granite walls up to thirty feet thick—as was the case at Couci in French Picardy—there was little danger that any enemy would break through. But there remained the problem of providing adequate access to the people who ought to be let in and out, while still maintaining defensibility.

A remarkable number of devices were used over the years to solve this problem. Perhaps the best known is the circular lake known as a *moat.* Comparatively few castles survive today with complete moats; most of them have silted up or been drained because of their unwanted impact on the foundations of the castles they surround. The Tower of London, for instance, once had a

mighty moat that is today a delightful grassy ditch used for strolls and picnics.

Two fully moated castles survive in Britain: Compton Wynyates and Bodiam. France has many in the Loire Valley, including Chambord, the hideaway of the infamous courtesan, Diane de Poitiers, Duchesse de Valentinois— mistress to two successive French kings.

And, although it may disappoint the child in each of us, there were no moats filled with alligators or loathsome creatures set to devour the unfortunate who fell in. Castles did empty their raw sewage into moats frequently— which would make swimming decidedly unappealing—and it also prohibited the survival of even very hardy wildlife.

Another solution to the entry problem was the *portcullis,* that mighty looking crosshatched gate that crashes down after the last defenders gallop back into Camelot from the field. It was a surprisingly effective means of defense, even though it did not give the protection that a solid wall (or solid door) might appear to give. Its advantages were that it deflected most arrows shot from the outside, but still allowed archers to shoot outward while hiding behind the massive beams that constituted its network of squares. At the same time, it was a fairly sturdy barrier, because it was lowered into place by a winch and was anchored on all four sides into stone ridges. A door, especially a double door, is weak in the middle, no matter how

E ven the strongest, most fearsome bastion was most vulnerable at its front door. The fortified gatehouse became an architectural fixation during the Age of Castles.

The variety of gateways is nearly as wide as the number of period castles themselves. They had, however, certain features in common. All gatehouses were constructed as attack towers: The castle defenders were able to mow down the entering knights from every angle. Many had archers' galleries at a number of different elevations.

Three sand interpretations of classic gatehouses.

A. A pierced portcullis is the dominant feature

of this twin-towered gatehouse. The entrance is surmounted by an arched walkway that is reminiscent of Queen Anne Boleyn's walkway at the Tower of London.

B. This plain gatehouse is on a model sturdy in construction and practical in battle. The conical roofs deflect arrows fired at the archers hidden at the tops. Even the archers' gallery over the gate is covered.

C. Looking as though it has been snatched from an archetypal Norman crusader castle, this heavily crenelated castle entrance is purely warlike in conception. It has a ruined look because it lacks doors, but its archway is technically impressive.

The concept that we all know as "castle" is a type of building that evolved in northern France as a response to Viking invasions in the Dark Ages. Normandy was especially hard hit by the Norse raiders—and it was repopulated by the descendants of Norse conquerors over hundreds of years.

The Norman castle is, at its simplest, a single round tower, or *donjon*, surrounded by a protective wall. The donjon, or *keep*, was from three to five stories tall—affording the advantage of height to archers in repelling attacks.

It was a crude affair, windowless and cold, dank and musty. And as civilization added new buildings to the castle complex, these central donjons were frequently abandoned for more comfortable quarters. Then, in the natural order of things, these most-fortified towers became strongholds for prisoners—what we now call *dungeons*.

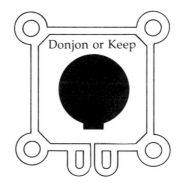

Donjon or Keep

Battlement or
Curtain Wall

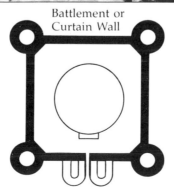

As the population grew in variety and complexity, castle lords frequently found it convenient to surround the donjon with an outer line of defense to protect the burgeoning village clustered around the walls of the keep.

The *curtain wall* as a concept dates from the time of the Crusades. When the semi-barbaric warlords of Europe saw Constantinople, they wanted to duplicate its walls at home.

The protected plaza within the curtain walls acquired the name of *bailey*. Its warden became a *bailiff*.

The curtain wall itself was frequently as thick as 10 or 15 feet. Since medieval siege warfare relied heavily on *mining* and *sapping* (digging holes under the walls to make them collapse), curtain walls frequently extended as much as 20 feet below ground level.

Many of the world's greatest castles are contained not within a single curtain wall, but within a series of them. The Tower of London, viewed from the air, is a box-within-a-box of stone curtains.

Gatehouses became the keys to defending permanent fortifications such as castles. They had to provide adequate access to friendly forces — but adequate defenses against invaders.

Double-towered gatehouses became the rule in major fortifications. In this arrangement, the defenders could station archers in both jutting towers to keep a wary eye on anyone entering.

The gate itself was usually given a chain-lowered gridded gate called a *portcullis,* which provided shelter for defenders, as well as good sightlines.

At some locations (Harlech Castle in Wales, for example), the fortifications of gatehouses were doubled: two smaller fortifications protruded in front of the already-jutting gatehouses themselves. The result was a small, controllable, nearly completely enclosed killing ground for unwanted visitors.

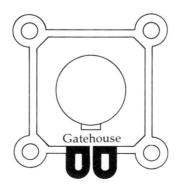

Gatehouse

Royal Windsor poses grandly amid the verdant foliage of Berkshire.

Windsor is a visual display of the development of the Norman castle. The original donjon built by William the Conqueror 900 years ago is still the most powerful feature, with the two later wings radiating out from it. The first curtain wall is still visible on two sides of the Round Tower.

Later embellishments — the designs and fancies of centuries of monarchs — have extended Windsor in two directions from the donjon. The closer is dominated by the Chapel of Saint George; the farther opens onto the medieval lord's most precious possession: the park.

erhaps the best-known aspect of castles in legend and song is the *moat*. Although they were not as widespread as fairytales and Arthurian myths would have us believe, they were a popular brand of defensive tactic.

Moats originated on the seacoast of Normandy and the Low Countries, where land could

be flooded with seawater at will. But the watery barrier was too good a defense for the warfare technicians of the Middle Ages to neglect.

This view of the ruins of Ragland Castle on the border between England and Wales shows the surviving moat with what must once have been very impressive hexagonal gatehouses.

massively it is bolted. A porticullis becomes, in effect, part of the impregnable wall it helps enclose.

But the most enduringly massive form of entranceway defense was the double gatehouse. It was perfected by the architects of Edward I of England during the conquest of Wales in the thirteenth century. One of the

most perfect still stands, although today it leads the visitor into a ghostly ruin that echoes past glory: Harlech Castle in Wales.

The double gatehouse was a tactical weapon as well as a defensive measure. A delegation from an enemy could be ambushed with impunity in the small enclosed area among the

four gatehouses at Harlech. The English Plantagenet monarchs were, on the whole, brilliant tactical warriors. Indeed, the flower of chivalry is always said to be represented by two of the most romantic of all the Plantagenets: the golden warrior, Richard the Lion-Hearted; and his great-great-nephew, Edward the Black

Prince. Of the handful of great knights whose names come down to us as ideal, shining-armor champions of chivalry, two spring from the blood royal of England. One—St. Louis IX—was a French king; no Spanish sovereign aspired to such recognition; no German monarch ever attained such distinction.

Architectural Embellishments

The people of the Middle Ages wanted things to look their best. They were successful in establishing styles of great grace, spirituality, and durability. Even if they had gone no further than the invention of the Gothic Cathedral and the medieval castle, they would have left their mark forever on Western civilization.

But they had brilliant decorative minds as well. And the stones of the castles that survive show their sophistication. Doorways, especially public doorways, were decorated with *orders* that appeared as sculptural borders. As the wealth and taste of castle dwellers improved, doorways came to be decorated with as many as eight concentric orders at once.

Windows in the Norman castle were typically *double-lighted* affairs, meaning they were a pair of tall windows side by side, frequently divided by an ornamental pillar called a *mullion*.

Many windows were *splayed*, or formed obliquely, so that the exterior edge of the window was considerably wider than the interior edge. This device gave greater range to window-positioned archers and made shooting an arrow into a window nearly impossible. To protect the

inhabitants further during a battle or siege, some windows were *double-splayed*—splayed on the top and bottom as well as the sides.

Virtually all donjons and almost all curtain walls were intersected at regular intervals by *pilaster buttresses* or flat columns that acted as structural supports and decorations. They look much like decorative columns to the casual observer and were treated as such in the later Middle Ages by the addition of fanciful capitals, flutings, gargoyles, and so on.

Most European castles were also decorated with one or more *stringcourses,* a term for a horizontal line that extends part- or full-way around a building. The name is obviously derived from the method of laying out such a decorative device, a method that still proves usable today. The builder stretches a line taut from one turret to another and marks off a horizontal line with chalk. That line is then built in some decorative mode by the masons working on the wall. In the case of a rubble wall, for instance, a stringcourse might be a horizontal row of herringboned bricks three-quarters of the way to the top. The process could be a laborious one, since walls took a full year to advance eight feet vertically.

Bricks were not commonly manufactured for castle-building, but castles were frequently located on the sites of former settlements. And if, as in many cases, that former settlement had at one time been a Roman villa or encampment, the mound would be full of baked clay Roman bricks. The walls at Ragland Castle in Wales, for instance, contain reused Roman bricks scattered here and there throughout the building. The rubble filling inside the hollow walls at Colchester has yielded piles of Roman coins bearing the image of Constantine the Great—obviously buried since the departure of the last Roman legions from Britain in the early part of the fifth century AD.

The great castles were always built for extremely practical purposes. But they were usually built by rough-and-ready, arrogant, aggressive people with extremely heady ideas of personal power. And each castle has a personality that imbues it—sometimes a series of personalities, each recognizable in a certain portion. Castles that were inhabited over many centuries are frequently a nearly unpardonable mélange of different styles. A quick glance at Compton Wynyates in England, for instance, shows styling from at least three entirely different architectural periods: Tudor, Neoclassic, and pure Gothic.

The way of life of five centuries can be gleaned from a day's tour of such great castles as Warwick, the Marksburg, Valladolid, Cracow, or Bran. And in doing so we see that the castle heritage left to the world is really a mute record of some of history's most influential personalities.

Although all castles were built for defense, no two castles are exactly alike. Likewise, no two sandcastles are alike in every detail. And it is in the detail that a castle replica "comes alive."

(1) an elaborate donjon or keep with a square gatehouse attached.

(2) drawbridge and ogive door viewed from the interior.

(3) castle facade with drawbridge and studded facing on the towers.

(4) hexagonal-roofed turret surmounting a corbelled battlement.

(5) cone-roofed oriel supported by a vertical plinth; arrow-slits or loopholes in each merlon.

(6) fine detail showing crenels, an arrow loophole, and a series of corbels supporting the parapet.

(7) a model castle combining a wealth of fine architectural embellishments.

(8) donjon protected by a small

shell wall that forms the focal point for a larger curtain wall.
(9) irregular hexagonal turret surmounting a curtain wall.
(10) square donjon elaborated by rounded pilaster buttresses.
(11-12) two varieties of decorative crenels, the second of which is underlain by a double stringcourse.
(13) a gate formed by a true Roman arch with a keystone.
(14) a fortified bridge for attacks against waterborne enemies.
(15) this square tower displays four fine oriels and a traditional Norman double-lighted window.
(16) a regal combination of ashlar and rubble in this wall segment.
(17) ogive window through a thick castle wall.
(18) archers' gallery.
(19) unusual drawbridge lowered by a single timber.
(20) interior view of fortified entrance of the type found in Crusader castles.

4

The Art of Sandcastling

Sandcastles are born in the imagination. They bring to life fantasies, legends, and myths standing on the borders of reality. They are best seen and best created through the mind's eye.

So the first essential ingredient is a dream. Of course, imagination by itself does not suffice. You must acquire the skills to match your dreams—or you will remain a bemused armchair sandcastler, nurturing pipe dreams of unfulfillable glory.

Fortunately the skills required for sandcastling are developed with reasonable ease in a pleasant environment. You may find that your only direct cost is an investment in suntan lotion. You may find an unwelcome extra portion of sand in your bathing suit. You may find that time slips maddeningly away from your

architectural endeavors. But the skills themselves will come fairly easily, fairly quickly.

And not all of it comes from playing in the sand. As with other artistic media, you have to know your materials and your environment before you can begin to create. You must get to know the beach, the tides, the sands. You must gather your tools. And you must learn the fine and ancient art of patience and concentration.

Tides
Tides are both friend and enemy to the sandcastler. Their repeated washings and poundings,

scraping the rocks of the ocean floor, have created the sands which enable beach sculpture. But that same eternal action is the eventual destroyer of sand art as it sweeps the beaches level and clean at high tide.

Because the science of predicting tides is so complex, most sandcastlers choose the easy way out: the local newspaper. Tidal information is usually included in the weather section, along with the sunrise and sunset times. The ideal timing for a day-long sandcastle endeavor is a high tide that occurs at about sunset. Then, if you choose your

61

site properly, you'll have the whole sunny day to build and you'll be able to watch the watery devastation of your efforts just as the sun sinks, casting its bloody glow across the advancing waters.

There's a strong compatibility between the dying of the day and the destruction of sandcastles; there's a poignancy, a sweetness to it that makes the experience breathtaking.

Finding the Tide Line
Because you'll want wet sand to build with, you'll need to locate the tide line on the beach. The good, buildable, wet sand will be between the tide line and the water's edge. The closer you get to the water's edge, the wetter will be the sand.

But tied to the need for wet sand is the need for time; you'll want all of it you can get before marauding waters come to claim their prize. And that's where locating the tide line becomes important.

The tide line is a mark along the sand that tells you the point to which the tides reach at their very highest. If you plan to build on the tide line, you can be assured of wet sand and of maximum time between high tides.

Tide lines are marked on different beaches in different ways, but there are some keys that are almost universal. The first is wave markings. The front edge of a wave is usually a frothy, foaming line of white water, and as that front edge licks the sand and disappears back into the ocean, it will leave a nearly imperceptible line of broken sand bubbles along the beach. From low tide to high tide, countless wave lines are

created, then destroyed, by successive waves—until the time of the highest tide.

Then one wave will reach farther onshore than any of the others. And the bubble line of that one wave will remain inscribed on the beach, a telltale, nearly invisible signal to the sandcastler that ideal sand and ideal timing coincide.

If you are planning, as most sandcastlers do, to build your edifice on a popular beach, locating the tide line is even easier. Just look for the area of the beach that has a smooth, almost glassy, appearance—and no footprints. As the tides come in, they smooth the beach to an almost clothlike finish. You'll notice some rippling where the wave action has been erratic, but you'll see a relatively virgin stretch of sand below the tide line.

You'll also see beach joggers favoring the sand below the tide line, because it is firmer and more compact. It's difficult to run in the sand above the tide line; it's tough on the ankles.

Choosing Your Building Site
Once you've located the tide line, you're ready to choose a site for your dream castle. Just like the castle builders of yore, you must ponder several criteria in choosing a site. First is the wetness of the sand. If you're in an area such

as Pensacola, Florida, which experiences only one change of tides daily, you'll have to check the sand at the tide line for wetness.

If you pick up a handful of sand and it refuses to hold together when you squeeze it, move closer to the water. If you pick up a handful and water runs out when you squeeze it, move farther away from the water. The trick is to find sand that is the consistency and wetness of well-cooked oatmeal. It should be too wet to sculpt in, but dry enough to pile up easily with a shovel. Remember that if you pick a sand that's too wet, you're going to break your back moving it. If you pick sand that's too dry, you're going to break your arms carrying buckets of water to the site.

After you're sure that you've found perfect sand, consider the flow of beach traffic and try to locate yourself away from the central crowds. If you attract too large a group of oglers, someone will have a dog that will run through your proudest tower in a frenzy of playful energy. All the apologies in the world won't rebuild your tower.

Don't locate yourself directly in front of a lifeguard tower. In an emergency, if your sandcastle lies in the lifeguard's path to a swimmer in trouble, you have no gripe coming. Lifeguards have a way of hosting motorized visitors as well—jeeps, trucks, dune buggies—which does not bode well for the sandcastler intent on his work. Even if they don't run over your masterpiece they splatter sand with considerable velocity as they drive by. And the

The most important thing for the sand-castler to keep in mind about tides is that they occur twice a day in most places: just short of twelve hours apart. So it's a good bet that at the lowest tide (pictured here), you'll have only about six hours of working time at the tide line before catastrophe strikes in the form of a killer wave.

The tide line itself can be recognized by the sand's texture (caused by foam left to dry), the spotty line of seaweed bits left by the highest waves, and the smoother texture of the sand on the ocean side of the tide line.

If you plan a multi-day castle event, be sure to build on the dry side of this line.

vibrations made by a dune buggy can pretty easily earthquake your castle flat.

The Drip Sandcastle

Perhaps the most uniquely sandy type of architecture is the method known as *dripping* a sandcastle. It is essentially a speeded-up version of a method favored by Nature herself, but usually not on beaches. Anyone who has visited the vast and spectacular Carlsbad Caverns, or the Oregon Caves, or the Caves of the Wind, has seen the shiny pallid spires that scientists call stalagmites. They are formed by a steady drip of mineral-rich underground water hitting a steady target over centuries. Each droplet carries a grain of calcite or aragonite, increasing the eerie tower by an unnoticeable mite.

The same principle applies to a dripped sandcastle—but *you* act in the place of the dripping water. The process in its simplest form yields a tower that looks something like a giant African anthill, but it can produce a surprisingly sophisticated structure very much in tune with certain schools of modern architecture.

To drip a sandcastle, you need only one tool: a bucket. You also need patience, because the process is very slow.

Fill your bucket halfway to the top with moderately wet sand. Be sure to search through the sand and remove any traces of seaweed, shells, or pebbles. What you will

be trying to create in your bucket is a mushy, homogenized mixture of sand and water that is roughly the consistency of cake batter or almost-whipped cream.

Dripped sandcastles are most successful when beach sand is very fine and mixed with a small amount of dredge or mud. A white coral beach is less than satisfactory, because white coral sand doesn't adhere to itself easily enough. Brown sands are the best for dripping. You can test the fineness of the sand easily.

Grab a handful of *dry* sand from above the tideline; hold it for a minute, then drop it. Examine your hand to see if it remains covered with sand. If it does not, give up on dripping. If the sand clings to your hand, then try flicking it off with a towel. The more the sand clings, resists

Brick sandcastle

Drip sandcastle

removal, the finer it is. And the finer it is, the better it is for dripping.

Sand does not dissolve when mixed with water. You can never achieve the consistency of mud with beach sand. The granules must be small enough to be held together by the surface tension of the water mixed with it. If it remains grainy and coarse when mixed with water, it will not adhere in castle form. You may achieve some wonderful ruins, but not a finished castle.

If you have the right kind of sand in your bucket, your next step is to fill the bucket to the brim with water from the next available wave. After doing that, check to remove seaweed and debris.

Reach into the bucket, through the water layer on top, and pick up a fat handful of sand. As you raise your hand out of the bucket, it will begin to drip out of your hand and back into the bucket. That's all right. You are saturating the sand with water as your hand passes through the water layer on top of the bucket, and you can expect to lose some in the process. Nobody, after all, ever said that dripping a sandcastle was quick.

When you have retrieved a handful of supersaturated sand, you're ready to begin. Hold your sand in a loose fist, with your thumb on the top. Form a cone with your hand, your little finger providing the closure. Now open the bottom of the cone by relaxing your little finger, and let the sand

run out in a steady stream.

If your sand is the right consistency and your hand is in the right position, the sand should run out in a thin and quite steady stream—no globs or heavy splats should escape.

The sand you're dripping should begin to set up and dry almost as soon as it hits the ground (if you are keeping the stream thin enough). Once you have achieved the required mastery of the technique, try it two-handed, either together or in rotary.

The rest is up to your imagination and to your developing skill. The experienced dripper can build towers that stand the height of a sizable Texan, and that possess the delicacy of a fairy kingdom. Since dripped sand dries more evenly and more quickly than molded or

Simple molded sandcastle

Sculpted sandcastle

sculpted sand, you can do some fascinating things that you might not be able to do otherwise. You can make a leaning tower, for instance, by simply moving your drip slightly to one side as the tower rises. You can build a zig-zag tower by moving the drip back and forth.

Your end product will usually look like a snow-hung fir tree, or an entire grove of them. But it can easily look like a futuristic city from some science-fiction dream: Martian, Venusian, or from a distant galaxy light years beyond the blackness of farthest space.

It will be hard to imagine that medieval princesses hang out in the halls of your big dripper—but medieval princesses don't hold an absolutely universal fascination anyway. Maybe there's an alien being, breathing cobalt-blue flames, pulsating slimily and evilly in the dank sub-basement of the highest tower.

Drip Technology

Drip sandcastles will remain forever bastions of handwork because each layer must dry before the next layer is applied. They cannot be speeded up, because if they are built too fast, they flatten themselves out into drip mounds.

There are, nonetheless, some technological innovations that can be added to the basic drip format to regularize the process. The first implement that can become useful is a large kitchen funnel. If you take a handful of sand in the same reaching-through-the-water manner, and drop it slowly into a funnel, you can, with some precision, drip the muddy sand exactly where you want it by aiming the funnel.

And if you want to get the

fundamentals of assembly-line technology working for you, the funnel will allow the roles of dripper and mixer to be separated. One worker can serve the function of funnel holder and construction planner, while the other (perhaps less fully trained) can mix sand and water to the desired consistency and be responsible for maintaining a steady flow of it.

In addition, a wide range of kitchen implements can be used to aid the dripper: spoons, basting suction droppers, cake decorating tools.

The careful browser will find many children's toys that can be of considerable use in dripping sandcastles. Prime candidates are tools for use in working modeling clay, playdough, or other mashable sculpture media. Most of these children's toys have the advantage of being washable, inexpensive, and resistant to the incursions of salt water.

One of the most moving and surprising works of modern art is Antonio Gaudí's masterwork, the Expiatory Church of the Sagrada Familia in Barcelona. Gaudí himself spoke of its fanciful "spars, masts, and sails."

Not far removed in spirit or execution, the masterful drip sandcastle seen here seems to combine the arching spirit of the high Gothic period with a startlingly futuristic vision.

Either could be a setting for the Ages of Castles — or for *The Martian Chronicles.*

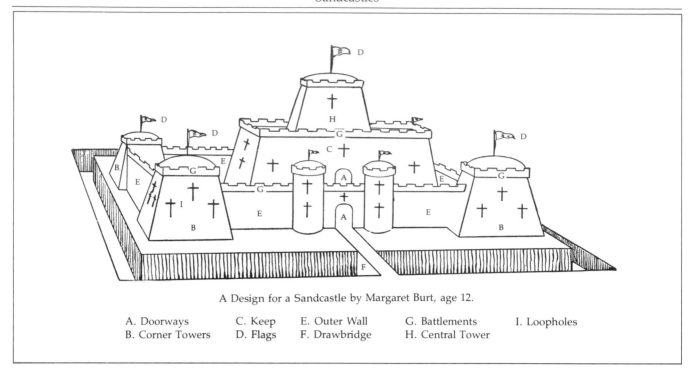

A Design for a Sandcastle by Margaret Burt, age 12.

A. Doorways   C. Keep   E. Outer Wall   G. Battlements   I. Loopholes
B. Corner Towers   D. Flags   F. Drawbridge   H. Central Tower

The Simple Molded Castle

If the dripped sandcastle is the easiest in technique, the molded castle is not far behind it. By far the most common method of sand construction, the simple molded castle is the hands-down winner of sandcastle popularity contests worldwide.

Molded castles are the ones favored by children with buckets and pails, and the principles of construction are not complex. Ingenuity in molding castles comes with an eye that is keen to the shapes of common molding devices. And the only really essential skills required are a pair of fast and steady hands.

To mold a sandcastle, select a container that is widest at the mouth and narrowest at the base. The basic paradigm of all sand molds is a paper cup: a cylindrical container with a top that is larger than the base.

Pack your selected container with wet sand: sand that is wet enough to *almost* run off the edge of a shovel—but not quite. Remember that the wetter the sand you work with, the longer your castle will last before it begins to fall apart from simple dehydration. But when you're molding a castle, you must use sand that is not the least bit soupy, or it will not hold a shape.

Inspect the sand, as you fill your container, to see that it does not contain any seaweed, shells, or other debris. Pack the container tightly with sand and smooth the top of the container with a flat edge.

Now prepare a flat surface to receive your tower. If you are going to build a *motte* and *donjon*

castle, pile up a *motte* with a flat top. You can round it off after your *donjon* is in place. The slightest unevenness in the receiving surface can cause a molded tower to crumble—if not now, then later when it begins to dry.

Then simply invert the sand-filled container onto the receiving surface—with lightning speed. Try to smack it down against the ground with a fairly strong thump, to loosen the sand from the sides of the container.

Pick the inverted container up—straight up, and slowly. If the sand does not slide out as you pick it up, tap it gently with your hand or with a tool. Do not twist the container. When you lift it up, voilà! a ready-made casting of the mold you chose.

The Right—and Wrong—Containers
The inventive molder can produce a sandcastle of quite amazing sophistication, simply by choosing

The *Chatterbox* castle finally came to life, over 100 years after it was designed by 12-year-old Margaret Burt. It has a childlike quality, and is entirely made by the simple molded technique. Even the crenelations were molded — with doll's teacups. Relatively period accurate, this simple molded castle's defenses are entirely in order.

his molds carefully. There are some common choices: plastic buckets, paper cups, cooking pots, gelatin molds.

Even without varying from these standard molds, quite a lot can be done. Towers can surmount towers, which in turn surmount other towers — provided, of course, that you have enough graduated containers to construct such a pile. Towers can surmount walls in close imitation of the medieval curtain walls.

But when a simple molded castle is cast from unusual molds, it can be a knockout. The more unusual the mold, the more unusual the product. A fluted kitchen trash can, for instance, produces a fluted tower. A shortening can produces a tower that is the same diameter at top and bottom—therefore a tower that can be stacked successfully.

One two-person operation that falls into the simple molded

category is the sliding mold. Take a shortening can and remove both ends. Be sure that you select a can that has no ridges anywhere in it. Beat down any rough edges with a hammer. Use tinsnips if necessary to remove any untoward roughness at the ends. Be sure to file the sharp edges.

Now one person holds the can on the sand, rotating it a bit from time to time to make sure that the sand does not adhere to it. As the can is filled up with sand by the second person, the tower mold is raised off the ground to deepen the cavity inside. Then the sand is added progressively higher, while the mold is raised progressively higher. The eventual effect of this is to create a mold of nearly

unlimited height but small diameter. But don't try it if you don't have a very steady mold holder—the least motion from side to side can topple the entire structure.

There are some types of molds that will not work well. No mold with interior bulges will work, because the inside diameter will be larger than the mouth. No mold with horizontal ridges in it will work, because the ridges will catch and scrape the sand as you remove it. Airtight molds are more difficult than those with "breathing" holes. Very large, closed-end molds are difficult as well.

If you plan to mold with a large container—a trash can, for instance—you will do well to cut it open by removing the bottom. Then the mold can be eased off the incipient tower by pouring water on the top of it. Such molds cannot be filled and upended either, of course. They must be made on the

Destruction can — in isolated instances — be a joy in itself. Here the two latter-day interpreters of Margaret Burt's castle blueprint enjoy a foot-stomping good time in a ritual that beaches across the world witness at sunset every day.

spot by filling them up and then removing them.

Containers with square corners, or with angles of less than ninety degrees, are apt to be problematical as well, because angles don't slide off as easily as do curved surfaces.

Open Molding
A technique that takes practice and several pairs of hands is what we call "open" molding. You create the mold in order to create the proper shape. To create a mold, look for interesting textures first. Try a piece of knotty plywood, for instance.

Now hold the plywood in place vertically by propping it up against something—or by getting your assistant to hold it. Then pile sand up against it and pack it tightly. When you've piled the sand up as high as you'd like to have it, remove the plywood. What you'll have left is a hill of sand with one smooth vertical wall.

By the same principle, and by the addition of a second piece of plywood, you can create castle walls in a manner remarkably similar to an early medieval method. Hold two plywood planks a few inches apart and plant them vertically in the sand. Now dump wet sand between them and pack it carefully. When you've finished packing the sand, remove the plywood planks— carefully. If you haven't been too ambitious and created a wall that's structurally unsound, the wall will stand proudly smooth on both sides. For additional structural reinforcement, slant the plywood sheets out a bit at the bottom; that tactic will allow you to build

additional height. And if anyone asks, just tell them you're putting the absolutely historically accurate sloping plinth at the bases of your curtain walls.

Now, at the corners of your long smooth wall, plant towers—big fat round ones. Then, because the towers are round, you can start another wall off in another direction without worrying about the corner join.

To avoid the unreal smoothness and sameness of most molded structures, try some imprint molding. Take some objects to the beach with you that have interesting textures. A used brick is a good beginning. Once you've erected your curtain walls, press the brick lightly into the sides, giving a mottled texture to your walls. A pierced egg-turner or kitchen spatula also gives an interesting wall texture.

For the fantasy castle of your dream, try using cookie cutters to

Discarded plywood sheets can become the basic molds of a thick and sturdy curtain wall, no hammer and nails required.

The technique is to hold two parallel flat surfaces steady and fill the area between them with sand (and water, of course). Then gingerly remove the flat molds to reveal a battle-ment that can be transformed into a Crusader's retreat, a Welsh citadel, or a medieval city stockade. *(below)* A sandcastler works on what appears to be an industrial complex. A gelatin mold has provided a perfect capital for the silo-like tower near the center of the picture.

imprint stars, bells, leaves, or other fancy shapes on your towers, your walls, and your gatehouses. A few cookie cutters and a generous dollop of ingenuity can lead to a magnificent witch's house from Hansel and Gretel.

To give an exotic look to your paper-cup or bucket towers, try using old teacups or coffee mugs as tower-capping molds. You can get a variety of interesting shapes from old teacups with broken handles. Some will have rounded bottoms (which become, of course, rounded tops when inverted); others will have squared bottoms. Some will be tall and skinny; others will be short and fat.

Even pasteboard or cardboard containers can be used, although they will not last long, of course. The boxes that contain long, skinny Christmas presents can make excellent wall molds.

For a touch of authenticity in your molded castle, take some twine to the beach with you. When your walls are complete, stretch the string tightly along the walls and cut slightly into the sand in a line running along the walls. What you're producing is a *stringcourse,* one of the most common exterior decorations of all medieval castles.

Formal gardens can be created with conical molds, such as the conical drinking cups made by several manufacturers. Authentic-looking splayed windows can be created by pushing the corner of a small square object into the walls of your keep or *donjon.*

In the final analysis, your molded castle will be as creative as you make it. It can take on the heroic dimensions of a city, or it can be a small, simple home typical of a lonely warlord. It can be as fanciful as Saladin's pavilion tents, or as plain as the early square tower at Oxford.

The Brick Castle

The least common type of sandcastle is made from a fairly standard building material: bricks. The difference here is that the bricks are made of beach sand—which makes for a painstaking but absolutely smashing product.

What you need to build a brick castle is a brick maker, a rectangular cast or mold. There is a variety of children's toys which might fit the bill—you have only to search the shelves of your local toy store for a likely tool.

If you're not the type to poke around in toy departments, try a wooden matchbox or any other small container of a similar shape. For an assembly-line approach, try using a plastic ice tray.

To make bricks, you'll want sand that is about the same consistency as bread dough. While you'll never get sand to adhere to itself as well as glutinous flour, you can aim for the same wetness and the same feeling. Then pack the brick molds with sand. Let them sit for a minute or two, then tap out your bricks onto a smooth, hard surface. A piece of plywood or a cookie sheet is an ideal brick-drying device.

What you're doing here is similar to a centuries-old technique practiced all over the world with remarkably little variation. But instead of mud and straw, you're using sand, which is a mite less permanent and a good deal more difficult to handle. But essentially what you'll be building with is adobe-style bricks.

Your next step is to plane out a large, absolutely flat surface. A good method is to take a broomstick or a piece of lumber and grade the earth with it until there are no valleys or hillocks left on your site. Be careful to replane or regrade every time you leave a footprint. A brick tower can collapse without warning if it is not level; after you've built one, you'll realize how disastrous that can be—because a brick tower represents a lot of sweat, suntan lotion, and concentration.

Once you have enough bricks (and this will depend on what you want to build and the size of the bricks you're manufacturing), line them up on a portable platform and transport them to the building ground. Then, like a mason or bricklayer, begin to arrange your bricks into walls.

A mason's trowel will serve to place the bricks in position; but there are some homier tools that will serve equally well. A common kitchen egg-turner is easily transformed into a sand mason's tool, as is a table knife. A short period of experimentation will suffice to show you how much pressure your bricks will take before they crumble. Some beaches will yield bricks that are sturdy enough to withstand being held between your fingertips. Other beaches—those with coarser sand—will give you bricks that seem to crumble at even slight pressure.

But take heart in one reassuring fact: The more you build, the less likely your building is to crumble. Even though the bricks themselves are not structurally sound, they carry the same advantages that regular housebricks do—they're considerably more sturdy than other methods of construction and they reinforce each other.

Once you have mastered the molded, the dripped, and the brick sandcastle, you can achieve some really astonishing effects by combining two or three of these techniques. You might choose to construct the turrets on your curtain walls out of bricks, for instance, while constructing the curtain walls themselves out of plywood hand-held molds. Then your donjon could be molded, with brick crenelations. Gothic spires can be added by dripping thick water-sand mixtures and creating tall, thin stalagmites.

Bricks of sand can be made with a number of different molds. These were made with a discarded children's toy the builders could not identify.

The result could be the desert stronghold of Harun al-Rashid, or of Beybars the Panther. It could be an outpost of the French Foreign Legion. One of the most painstaking and rewarding techniques.

The Sculpted Castle

The *pièce de résistance* of all sandcastles is the fine-artist's approach to the medium: the sculpted castle. It is the most time-consuming; it requires the most care and technique; and it is by far the most spectacular in possibilities.

The sand sculptor uses beach sand the way Rodin used bronze, the way Michelangelo used marble: as though there were a castle waiting within—calling out to be freed. All the sculptor needs is a well-compacted lump of sand and a few tools, and then his fantasy castle heaves into life as he locates it within the formlessness of a sand heap.

The first essential for a sculpted castle is a solid, workable mountain of sand. Since most beaches do not supply this ready-made, the first problem that the sculptor encounters is creating an extremely compacted medium. And make no mistake about it: If you skimp on compaction, disaster will inevitably follow. Tightly compacted sand is the only medium you can sculpt with.

Working with Forms

Creating a highly compacted pile of sand can be a tricky feat, but the approaches to it are legion. The necessary components—sand and water—are easy to acquire. And the most common technique is casting rough forms in dimensions suitable to the project at hand.

The forms themselves can be almost any shape and any size. Heroic castles, such as the Heidelberg profiled in Chapter 5, take heroic measures in preparation, most often in the form of heavy machinery: tractors and road-grading equipment.

But we assume that most castles are smaller than Heidelberg, which contained upwards of 2,500 tons of sand. Less drastic preparations are required. A common method is constructing casts similar to those used in pouring cement—casts which are both easy to make and entirely reusable.

One versatile set of casts involves three concentric squares, which are piled up to form a step-pyramid shape on the beach.

Circular casts can be put together quickly and easily from sheets of acrylic plastic. If two ends of a sheet of pliable plastic or formica are joined, the material will form an almost perfect circle automatically. Such plastic can be

transported to the beach flat—in stacks—and assembled on the spot.

Large plastic containers, such as trash cans, are suitable for towers and turrets, but they should have both ends open (which means cutting off the bottom). Plastic piping, such as that used for

plumbing sewer connections, can be purchased at any plumbing supply store or hardware store.

Once you have selected your casts, you are ready to begin creating your base material. The rule to keep in mind is that the larger molds are put in place first, while the smaller ones are put in place progressively later.

Next to your molds, your most essential tools will be buckets, because you will have to move considerable amounts of water from the shore line to your building site. The more buckets you can get, the better off you'll be. It is a good idea to fill them all to the brim before you put your first cast in place—so you won't spend your time running back and forth to the surf when you should be casting.

Casting the Forms

Grade the beach site you have chosen so that it is as close to flat and level as you can get it. Then place your first (that is, your largest) mold on the flat area you have prepared. If you have brought a carpenter's level with you, so much the better.

Next, spray the inside of your mold with a Teflon-type cooking spray. This will help you in removing the molds later on; the sand will be less inclined to stick to the mold. If you are using corner-joined molds with detachable sides, the Teflon spray is not essential.

Then dump several buckets of water into the molds, ideally enough to fill the mold nearly halfway with seawater. A hose connected to a faucet will not help, as seawater bonds sand better than fresh water does. An assembly-line approach to water-bearing is useful, though—and an excellent way to "break in" first-time workers to the rigors of sandcastling.

The really big sand projects use hand-operated pumps to bring water to the site, but smaller projects usually have to make do with buckets.

Once you have half-filled the mold with seawater, position your champion stomper in the middle of the mold. A stomper is a barefooted person who acts as a human ground pounder, compacting the sand and water that you shovel and pour into the mold.

Then it's "bombs away" as you

Graduated forms of the same general shape are a multi-purpose beginning for a sculpted castle.

Here a pair of sandcastlers work with three square forms with bolted corners designed to snap apart eas-ily. Any number of different castles can be hiding inside the prosaic "layer-cake" form. A segment of 12-inch plastic pipe will be added to the top after the forms are compacted.

throw sand into the mold as quickly as possible, to use the most of the seawater's bonding power. Be sure to keep the sand-water mixture as soupy as possible throughout the mold. As more and more sand is piled into the mold, the stomper will rise higher and higher, until he or she is standing on top of it at finish.

Alternate methods of compaction remove the stomper and substitute a team of sledge hammers. If you elect to use the sledge-hammer approach, concentrate particularly on the edges and the corners of the mold first. It will be a slow process, but you will get maximum compaction—which you'll need if you're going for great detail.

Particular attention must be paid to the corners of square-cornered molds. If the corners are not filled first, the water you carry will run out in great disappointing rivers, much increasing the water-bearing detail's continuing burden.

If you plan to use more than one mold in pyramid fashion, do not remove the sides of the first mold until you are entirely finished with everything above it. Simply place the next mold on top of the first one and repeat with water/sand/stomping process for each successive mold.

You'll occasionally have a bit of

An intricate spire has appeared where once only a cylindrical column of sand stood. One of the sandcastlers mists the structure with a plant sprayer to keep it workable.

All sculpted sandcastles appear from the top down — never from the bottom up. You must imagine that your castle already exists inside the sand. You are simply freeing it from the sand that surrounds it.

resistance from one-piece molds, such as trash cans, piping, and buckets. They have very little "give" in them, and as you pack and stomp (or pound) the sand

into them, the sand adheres to the mold, no matter how much Teflon was used at the beginning. If the mold is a sizable one, it can become very difficult to make it "let go" of your molded sand.

If you find that your one-piece molds are sticking, try pouring a bucket of seawater through the top opening as you lift up on the mold. The lifters will be a bit wet, but the liquid will probably free the mold. The product of such a dousing may not be a beautifully shaped mold, but it is wise to consider that the shape is only there to be carved and whittled away—so the drips and gouges of

cruel fate probably don't make any real difference in your final product.

Remember as you mold that the gross shape of your molds need not dictate the shape of your final castle. A square mold can easily become a round tower when it is carved, and a round mold can be a square tower (just slice off the edges). A single mold can become two towers if the middle is removed. What you are creating is a medium you can work in. That's where sculpted castles differ from the simple molded ones we discussed earlier.

With simple molded castles, the mold you use is the shape you live with. With sculpted castles, the molds you use are usually not closely related to the final product—no more so than the block of marble looks like the Greek statue it gives birth to.

Sculpting Tools
The tools a sand sculptor uses are adapted from the tools used by fine-art sculptors who work in soft media such as clay or wax. But you need not spend time or money in an art-supply house to assemble a complete array of sand sculpting tools.

A quick raid of the kitchen utensils and a lightning sally through a basic workshop will do just fine. And since no harm will come to the tools, they can be returned to their original purposes as soon as the dying sun and the resurgent tide do their nasty work with your castle.

Remember, as you select your tools, that you will be going through two processes in building a sculpted castle: rough-cutting

An onion-shaped dome begins to take shape under the influence of a practiced hand and a kitchen measuring spoon.

With some expert care and a very steady hand, the dome takes on the swirls of holy Russian church architecture. It is finally lifted (very gingerly) and transported to its place on top of a nearby tower.

and final-detailing. In rough-cutting, you carve out the essential shapes you will be working on: the towers, the basic buildings, the walls. In final-detailing, you will add the intricacies that make your castle a dreamland: windows, columns, balconies, chimneys, staircases, corbels, stringcourses, flying buttresses, ornate doorways—even people.

Each of these processes requires a special type of tool. The rough-cutters use bulkier and rougher instruments. A putty knife is an indispensable rough-cutting tool, as is a flat-edged mason's trowel.

Final-detail work requires the most inventive selection of tools. The corbels along the top of the castle wall, for instance, can be created with a melon scoop. Windows and doors can be carved with a cake icer. Crenels can be cut with a table knife and lifted out of the solid wall with a spatula. All tools used for final detail must have easily gripped handles to give your wavering hand maximum control.

Do not try to work from formless lump straight through to finished castle. Part of the rough-cutter's task is to determine whether or not the structure will stand. It is a heartbreaking shame to put all the tracery on one side of a castle only to have it collapse when the other side is rough-cut.

The Great Challenges
Once you have mastered the tools and the basic techniques of compaction, you can create some castles that will leave the beachside oglers breathless. And you will be tempted to do some grandstanding (perfectly

With only the bottom form now remaining, most of Saint Basil's Cathedral has been freed from the captor sand.

The spires are detailed, but the area once covered by the middle form is only rough-cut. All the domes are in place. The sandcastlers close in for the grand finale.

understandable).

The legendarily difficult details are not necessarily the ones that might occur first to the bystander. Arches—see-through arches—are a mighty beginning. Prize-winning castles nearly always have arches that seem to defy gravity as it normally applies to sand. But arches are not the twinkling jewels in the sandcastler's crown.

What is an arch, after all, when compared to a portcullis that refuses to close—hovering several

All three forms have now been removed from Saint Basil's, and the cathedral that graces Moscow's Red Square is largely complete.

The continuous misting is more important than ever, as the fine-detailing process puts all the finishing touches on. The sculptor in the foreground creates a ramp that will become a staircase.

inches off the ground?

And there is no comparison between a single arch and an arcade of archways—with a formal garden on top of them!

Sandcastles are such a short-lived art form that they deserve as much glory and as much daredevil bravado as they can get. To quote one sandcastler overheard muttering to herself on a sunny beach in Southern California, "No sandcastle is finished until the doors have doorknobs and hinges." Now that's a tall order!

Teaching diagrams inspired by the sandcastle classes of journeyman sandcastler, Gary Kinsella, of Cardiff-by-the-Sea, California.

1. A tower must already exist inside your inverted-bucket mound of sand. You have simply to free it of the sand that does not belong.

2. Always sculpting with an upward motion, create the roofline.

3. Free the walls, leaving enough sand at the base for a staircase.

4. By carving straight in and lifting out the debris on your knife, create a roof overhang. Fine-detail your windows.

5. The undercutting process that will enable you to create realistic corbels.

6. Carve a smooth rampway where your staircase will be.

7. Beginning at the top of the staircase, incise a number of evenly spaced downward cuts on the ramp. Then lift the sand off each step from the front.

8. The finished tower, now connected to a curtain wall. Fine detailing has given us a doorway, windows, and a stringcourse.

The road to fantasy beckons the viewer of this heroic sandcastle built on Memorial Day weekend in 1980.

The pierced portcullis that bars entrance at the magnificent double-towered gatehouse is a major sandcastling feat—a seeming contradiction of the nature of sand as a medium.

Beyond lies a dreamlike castle on a hill, a home fit for Cinderella's prince, or for any medieval king. The splendor of this sand edifice is undeniable—and breathtaking.

The central keep of this sand wonder is a many-towered, many-turreted, palatial castle that seems to reach toward the skies in its ambition.

A square tower contains a sandy version of one of the Middle Ages' finest creations: a rose window.

The cool interior of this sandcastle seems to lie just beyond our vision as we gaze into the perfectly cut windows. A grand staircase leads ever upward toward the highest point, and a double row of corbels links pilaster buttresses that end in conical turrets.

The detailing of this Memorial Day castle becomes more awesome the closer one looks. Here a series of steps leads up to a version of the flying buttresses that graced Gothic cathedrals.

The perfect castle—the one that looms in the misty imagination of every sandcastler on every beach in the world—must look something like this. It looks real; every detail has been seen to, including the rocky look of the sand mound beneath the building, which was washed carefully to give the appearance of granite outcroppings. Nearly 2000 hours of work were invested in this grand image.

5
Heidelberg

Heidelberg. The site of one of the oldest universities in the world. The home of Sigmund Romberg's famous *Student Prince.* One of the most scenically magnificent cities in Europe. Perched on the banks of the Neckar River in Baden-Württemberg, Heidelberg is one of the last medieval cities that survives with its spirit—and its look—intact.

Not that it has had a peaceful existence these last 2,000 years. It was first settled by Roman soldiers in the period of Julius Caesar's Gallic Wars. Heidelberg has been inhabited continuously for more than twenty centuries.

Heidelberg Castle, now in ruins, was once one of the showplaces of the Black Forest, and is entwined in the histories of nearly all the nations of Europe. The British crown passed this way when the last of the Stuart monarchs died in 1714.

But still, as you visit it today, its winding streets speak of centuries of students—for learning has been the soul of Heidelberg for the most recent 600 years. There was a time when the most expensive and well-respected physicians in the world were proud to display Heidelberg credentials.

Heidelberg Castle was an architectural mongrel, the toy of successive generations of kings, dukes, archbishops, electors and princes. Some sections speak to the viewer darkly of the Middle Ages; neighboring towers—ablaze with sunlight from a hundred windows—seem to be the picture of the Renaissance predilection for light.

And this grab bag, this charming collection of architectural grandeur and folly, lived again—briefly—on a sunny beach in, of all places, Southern California. Gothic, Renaissance, and Golden Glory met the Pacific Ocean in a townlet called Cardiff-by-the-Sea in north San Diego County.

The project would include Heidelberg Castle—completely. It

would include a cathedral, a formal French garden with topiary plantings (made of sand), towers, turrets, French windows, piazzas, balconies, and statues. The onlookers would swear, by project's end, that the builders intended to mold period furniture to decorate the interiors.

Led by an architect and an architectural designer, a team of forty people would labor for four days from dawn until dusk to bring this fantasy out of the level sands, in the end investing nearly 2,000 work hours in a project as ephemeral as any the world has ever seen.

The finished replica of Heidelberg would contain nearly 2,500 tons of sand and would be nearly half the size of a football field! But all that was in the future as a bulldozer made its symmetrical tracks in the sand.

What began to take shape as the bulldozer did its methodical work was an artificial island a few feet offshore at the mouth of the river. As was the case with many medieval fortresses, it was connected to the mainland by a thin causeway of *terra firma*. And the island began to grow higher and higher.

Before long the bulldozer grew a huge steel arm and claw, giving it the appearance of a gigantic metallic praying mantis. And then the piling-up process began to go quicker as the scooping-and-piling raised a sizable islet out of the water. It was still an odd setting for a German castle, but the in-

trigue ingredient was beginning to draw a considerable crowd of well-wishers. For by now the master builders were beginning to assemble into teams of workers.

The sandcastler's first task (as we mentioned in Chapter 4) is to compact the sand into a usable medium, one that will not collapse as soon as it is carved. And here was the first real collaboration of man and machine—handwork and machine-made brawn.

Long sheets of plastic appeared from a caravan of car and station-wagon trunks, and enough five-gallon buckets to water the Bonneville Salt Flats. A team of bright-eyed grunts began filling the buckets with the abundant seawater that surrounded the project on three sides. The siting had been carefully planned to provide easy access to building materials.

The sheets of plastic, which were shaped like elongated rectangles, were equipped at each end with sliding doorlocks. They were then snapped quickly together into circles and ellipses and placed on the shapeless mound of sand that the bulldozer and powershovel had piled up.

The forms were half-filled with

seawater from the bucket brigade's standing supply, and a burst of feverish activity began, with a contest seeming to emerge between the bucket handlers and the sand handlers: Who could supply their ingredients quicker? The diesel engine of the bulldozer puffed and chugged as great scoops of sand were dumped into the molds.

And then the pounding began.

The sand had to be compacted, squeezed together, pounded until it was, virtually, as solid as rock. Sledge hammers were relied upon to do the job, and thus became the order of the day. Choruses of work songs cropped up from time to time as the teams of pounders swung those sledges, crashing them into the soft sand. And slowly the sand sank lower and lower, compacting into itself. More sand was added and the process began again. By the end of the first day of construction, the mound was ready. As the sun went down, the sand was once again drenched with seawater to finish the compaction process.

Guards were posted and barriers thrown up to keep the marauding tides away.

As the sun arose on the second day, the Heidelbergers were already preparing their tools for the day's work, shivering and drinking boiled beach coffee, for many of them had spent the night on the sand, bonfires lighting the night.

The second day was devoted to the process of rough-cutting: whittling the mounds of sand down to recognizable architectural

shapes. Period woodcuts, which were to be the master plans, were posted on stakes around the building site, and a considerable amount of discussion ensued about how to scale the buildings so that each would be in proportion to all the others. An approximate scale was agreed upon and the rough-cut team captains assembled the troops. The building process had begun.

Already the sandcastlers, as they stared at the sand mounds that would become Heidelberg, had begun to reject the follies of the real world and to regress in time. Their eyes did not seem to focus on the rest of the beach, nor on the chapparal-covered hillsides that ringed the project, nor on the crowds of well-wishers who had gathered early to watch the city emerge. Their focus was on the work of their hands, the age-old pride of the artisan conquering even the beach, the sun, and the inviting surf.

The forms were removed from the mound, and the landscape was, for a few moments, like a tank farm. Tools were gathered: trowels, putty knives, sheets of stiff plastic that would act as cutters, straight-bladed shovels, and kitchen knives.

It could not have been much different when the castle was first built. A hive of workmen must have swarmed about in a similarly aimless-looking manner, laying foundations, solving small catastrophes. Of course the time frame would have been much different,

because Heidelberg Castle was built over a period of several hundred years, while this project was scheduled to last only a few short days. It was like a telescoping of history: to be able to see an entire city arise from the sand, and eventually to see it collapse.

Slowly the castle, and the small city that surrounded it, began to take shape, the tops of the towers and rooflines clearly recognizable above the shapeless sand that would eventually become its lower stories.

The castle was founded by Louis I in the early years of the 13th century; it was enlarged by Rupert I two hundred years later, and then again by the Imperial Elector Frederick the Victorious in about 1453—as Johann Gutenberg was printing the first book ever printed in movable type in nearby Nuremberg. The palatial parts of the castle were added by Rennaissance Counts and Electors during the 17th century, when two historic events shaped the subsequent history of the city.

The first was the invasion of Heidelberg by the French armies of Louis XIV, the fabulous king who styled himself "Le Roi Soleil," or "The King with the Bril-

liance of the Sun." In 1688, the town capitulated to Count Mélac, the French general. Mélac held the city for only about six months before retreating—and blowing up the fortifications of the castle. Despite restoration over the next five years, the castle was again sacked and largely destroyed by Marechal de Lorge, another French conqueror, in 1693.

The final blow was administered by nature herself. Heidelberg Castle was struck by lightning in 1764. It has never been restored.

The second historic event of the 17th century was the connection of the Heidelberg ruling family with the English royal family. The ill-fated Frederick V married the eldest daughter of James I of England. It was from this marriage that England eventually inherited a Hanoverian royal family, beginning with George I in 1714.

Henceforth for 150 years, Heidelberg would be culturally allied to the northern European powers—rather than to the Catholic Bavarian sovereigns who had been her traditional alliances. Heidelberg University gained luster and international standing once again in 1804 when the Oxford-educated Grand Duke Charles Frederick of Baden endowed it with its world-famous scientific collections. Today no university library in the world is complete without the priceless scientific heritage of the "cradle of German science."

And by a strange series of circumstances, Heidelberg managed

On a small spit of land jutting out from San Elijo Lagoon, one fine morning joggers and beach residents saw a peculiar sight. A bulldozer was making its way off Pacific Coast Highway and onto the beach, just like an early-morning bather.

It lumbered slowly across the flat, white sand and then began a seemingly nonsensical grading project. Back and forth it chugged, pushing the warm sand this way and that, in a display of what must have seemed to the astonished onlookers a case of summer madness.

This out-of-place piece of modern technology was helping to create the setting for an ageless work of fantasy. As it plowed through the mushy sand at the water's edge, it was creating the underpinnings of a castle long deserted—and 7000 miles away. A group of sandcastlers had decided to embark on the most ambitious sandcastle project ever attempted. What would rise on the spot turned out, four days later, to surpass even the wildest expectations. Seventeenth-century Heidelberg would be reconstructed in such remarkable detail that the fat burghers of the Heidelberg Renaissance would have known each doorway, each window, each column.

to survive the ravages of the Industrial Revolution. It was never consumed by smokestacks and railroad tracks, manufacturing plants and coal mines. Like a few blessed towns here and there throughout Europe, it kept its charm unblemished by the passage of time.

And on a Southern Californian beach it enjoyed a new Renaissance, a chance for the world to see it as it was when it was younger, more important, more prestigious. A chance to imagine the streets peopled with nobles bedecked in feathers, jewels, and multicolored ribbons in the style of Versailles.

It was at Versailles, for instance, that the world became fascinated with what were then called "French" gardens. In the French garden, nature was entirely subjugated to the dictates of art. So bushes that would normally have grown into trees were kept clipped and trimmed into charming geometrical shapes—so that they could be balanced by other shapes, *each exactly the same,* at other locations in the perfectly symmetrical garden. The garden in this reconstruction of Heidelberg was one such; the bushes were all perfect balls, perfect cones, or perfect pyramids. Those perfect shapes were not there for the ease of the sandcastler, but were accurate reconstructions of the gardening styles of the day.

From a bravura standpoint, the potential sandcastler will be interested to note that the entire formal garden stood on a piazza

that was undercut by twenty arches, each of them deep enough to give the impression that they receded into a complete arcade. And the entire garden was surrounded by a balustrade in the Italian style, pierced through every two or three inches in absolutely regular fashion. The music pavilion at the end of the garden was designed as a retreat for the ladies of the court, in the same fashion as the Petit Trianon would be built for the doomed Marie Antoinette of France a century later. It was a chance to get away from ceremony, to put their feet up, and to indulge in gossip and giggling.

In contrast to the comforts of court life stood the dignified and beautiful Heiliggeist Cathedral, begun at the end of the fourteenth century, at the time of the founding of the university in 1386. It survived the religious wars of Catholic vs. Protestant, several times changing hands (and religions). Today it is a Protestant house of worship, but its architectural origins are unmistakably medieval and Catholic.

As a sand achievement, this cathedral was almost without parallel, even compared to the Heidelberg project, the most extensive sandcastle ever built. Its mammoth front door was ornamented with three entirely separate orders of decoration. All its windows duplicated the stone tracery of the original, although it lacked the stained glass of the original. Even the edges of its finely planed roofs were decorated with the tiny serrations of the original.

Like every castle, Heidelberg was originally built for purposes of defense—to withstand siege warfare. To do that, it had to have its own source of water: a spring within the castle walls. A series of waterwheels cascaded down the side of the castle in an early experiment with water power. It is not by water alone that we live—and in Heidelberg water was harnessed to grind wheat into flour The sandcastlers who carved the upright discs that became wheels needed granite-firm hands, and a lot of trial-and-error experimentation.

The rough-cutters who worked on the donjon carved the ancient Dicke Thurm as a smooth-roofed building, working conscientiously for a perfect conical shape (they succeeded). Then the finishing touches were added in the form of architectural stone spirelets that ran in vertical rows up to the apex of the finished building.

Heidelberg's famous Karl Theodor Bridge spanned the invisible Neckar River in the foreground of the sandy city—with copies of the original fortifications still in place. The arches in the bridge were complete: pierced through the structure. The spans of the bridge actually supported themselves on pilasters of pure sand.

A Labor of Glory
Why would forty normal people—many of them professionals in "real" life—devote four days of dawn-to-dark, back-breaking labor to building Heidel-

The builders of the real city of Heidelberg had the advantage of working with stone, brick, and mortar. The sandcastlers who would duplicate the original had to make crumbling beach sand the consistency of granite in order to support the delicate archways, the balustrades and balconies,

and the flying buttresses of Heiliggeist Cathedral.

The model was drawn from seventeenth- century woodcuts, from the period when Heidelberg's Count Palatine was powerful enough to win the hand of England's Princess Elizabeth, the eldest daughter of James I of England, Scotland, and Wales.

berg? After all, the nature of a sandcastle is such that you know when you begin that it will not last. If the replica had been done in balsa and durable materials, the purpose would have been different. But sand is such a short-lived medium! Why use it?

Sandcastles are not necessary to the sustenance of life—but what is life without a sense of wonder? of awe? of joy? And who can find fault with the sandcastler, any more than with the ballerina, the French chef, the pianist, or the baseball player who hits a home run? Each is engaged in creating a moment of triumph, a moment of splendor and personal achievement. The fact that that moment must end is of little importance—except that it makes the moment sweeter.

The sandcastler who slaves to achieve a moment of satisfaction, a moment of really completing something for once, a moment of exhausted pride, that sandcastler is joining the ranks of a select group of human beings.

How many of us can say we have ever been in a position to stand back and say, "There. That is finished, and that is mine, and I am pleased." What more reward can a person want than that ultimate satisfaction?

As you look at the workers in these pictures, note the fascination with which they worked. It was a peculiarly solitary form of teamwork, each artisan his own severest judge. Aside from the sounds of tools and the roar of the onlookers, a sandcastling site is a surprisingly quiet place, as each of the workers disappears into his task in a cloak of concentration.

There are no tangible rewards to be gained from building sandcastles of this sort. They take days out of lives; they expose the builders to salt air and sunshine; they cause aching backs and sore muscles. But it is precisely because there are no rewards to be gained that they are worthwhile. There are no "ulterior" motives in sandcastling; each worker is there for his or her own personal reward. Each worker will eventually be able to link arms with all the others and cheer proudly, "There. We did that. We did it and we're glad and proud and tired. But for once in our lives, we played the glory side."

As for the sandcastle itself, it lasted nearly four days after it was finished. But the sea reclaimed it—as it always will.

Conrad of Hohenstaufen, the Count Palatine, selected Heidelberg as his capital in 1155. The formerly insignificant town became a city of magnificence and continued to be the focal point of the Palatinate for 500 years, until the Imperial Elector Charles Philip transferred the capital to Mannheim in 1721, following a century of conflict.

In 1802 Heidelberg became a possession of the Grand Duke of Baden, who held it until the founding of the Weimar Republic in 1918.

Like a city that has been flooded and then frozen, Heidelberg appeared from the top down—a process that is peculiar to sandcastling and to architectural excavation (which this resembles in many ways). The rooftops were the first shapes that were at all recognizable. Then walls appeared beneath them—plinths, doorways, and roads.

Here and there a small collapse devastated the work and necessitated frantic repairs. But this team was nothing

if not well-prepared. Molds of all conceivable shapes and sizes seemed to appear as if by magic when needed. They had planned well. In addition to the enormously versatile sheets of plastic that were used for the larger molds, they had buckets of all sizes, PVC piping, garbage cans with the ends cut out, square wooden molds that snapped apart at the corners—a mold or a tool for every occasion.

Heidelberg, as it was in the early years of the seventeenth century, begins to take shape as (*top*) rough-cutters shape the major buildings of the city.

A sand artist (*below*) uses a cake icer to add final detail to the windows of the Dicker Tower, the original keep founded by Rupert I in about 1214. These windows pierce the outer shell in carefully measured four-pane segments. Even now, though, the lower parts of the tower have not been freed from the captor sand.

Rough-cutting begins at the top of the Achteckiger Thurm, a tower that appears to be a corner section of the original curtain wall that protected the plazas and gardens of the interior.

The shaping of the outline of the building is done with a mason's trowel here, but even at this point the oddly rounded octagonal roofline has been delineated.

94

The palatial residences of the castle take shape. In the top photograph, the plain Elisabethbau is seen on the right. It was built as a gift of love from Frederick V for his lovely English wife, Princess Elizabeth.

The ornately columned building is the Friederichsbau, which dates from 1601. Its three stories are of late Renaissance design. The worn statues were originally 16 likenesses of famous monarchs, from Charlemagne to Frederick IV. In this sandcastle the columns were molded off-site and transferred to the castle during the fine-detailing process.

Attention to fine detail at the sand Heidelberg was nearly perfect —inhibited only by the inadequacies of the sand.

Even at an early stage, the replica of the Friederichsbau (*top*) was impressive. Later the stories would be

ornamented with tiny columns, Corinthian capitals, and a series of statues.

The formal garden of Heidelberg's Gross Terrace (*bottom*) was true to the ''French'' garden style, with an Italian balustrade pierced every few inches for 10 feet. The original was built in 1613.

Karl Theodor (1742-99) was the Imperial Elector who built the magnificent bridge and gatehouse that today bears his name.

The sand Karl Theodor Bridge had a series of minor collapses—one is shown in the photograph below. Eventually patience and hard work won the day.

The fine detailing of all the buildings withstands even a close-up look. The windows at the top are from the Dicker Tower, Heidelberg Castle's oldest (700 years) tower.

97

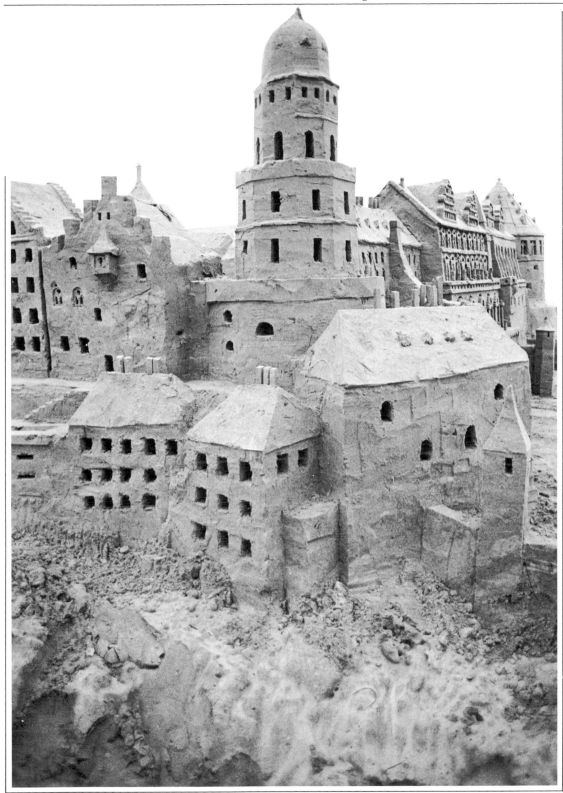

Two views of the east facade of the castle. *Opposite:* The view from the castle garden toward the front of the castle (showing Apotheker Tower) along a portion of the original curtain wall (largely destroyed to make way for residences). Both the corner towers are parts of the original fortifications erected by medieval Electors.

This page: The Achteckiger Tower is the crux of this view of the eastern and northern faces of the castle. The northern face (to the right) is toward the Neckar River and is usually thought to be the "front." The chimneys, the stepped roofs, the windows, the stringcourses, the terraces, the balconies—all are faithful to the set of Renaissance woodcuts that guided the project.

Much of the detail seen in this sand Heidelberg does not exist in reality; it was destroyed by a French army 300 years ago.

One of the most intricately carved sand sculptures ever attempted, this replica of Heidelberg's Heiliggeist Cathedral (Holy Ghost Cathedral) was a monument of awe even to the expert sand-castlers who built Heidelberg Castle.

The ten crosses that decorate it were molded off-site and transferred to their pinnacles. The decorations of the orders around the front entrance were painstakingly added piece by piece. The lat-ticework in the bell tower is double-layered. A cathedral worthy of its double.

Smaller buildings were given the lavish attention that might easily have been directed only toward the heroically sized ones. The detailed buildings (*top*) were not even visible from the front of the castle, but fidelity to the period was followed to the last degree.

The Music Pavilion (*bottom*) was built as a retreat from the formality of court life by Frederick IV in 1613. Many of Germany's most illustrious musicians must have played here in Heidelberg's heyday. From a bravura standpoint, the pavilion sits atop a plaza that itself is undercut by no fewer than 24 round arches.

This sweeping panorama of the front of Heidelberg Castle shows much of the castle proper, together with a portion of the now-destroyed city wall. The major buildings of the Renaissance city are visible in the foreground, with the northern face of the castle prominent in the background.

Building a gargantuan sandcastle such as this is as much an exercise in organization as in sand-sculpting skill. Even though the city appears as a unified whole, it was built by a team of forty people working in close harmony. *Bravissimi!*

6

Longen to Goon on Pilgrimages

When the warm winds of spring began to breathe life back into the land emerging from winter, when the flowers bloomed in riots along the hedgerows, the people of the Middle Ages began to yearn for travel. Not unlike the folk of today, the renewal of spring each year made the populace long to be footloose and fancy-free. But where the modern family might decide on a vacation, the medieval counterpart often decided to go on a pilgrimage.

The title of this chapter is a phrase from *Canterbury Tales* by Geoffrey Chaucer, who chose to place his great literary work on the road to Canterbury, the most popular pilgrims' destination in England for nearly 400 years. It was the tomb of the martyr-saint, Thomas Becket, who had been murdered in his cathedral at the behest of Henry II in the middle of the twelfth century. One of the richest shrines of Christendom,

the martyr's tomb at Canterbury was decked with gold and jewels given by pious pilgrims over the centuries. It was finally despoiled in the sixteenth century by another Henry—Henry VIII—who stripped it of all its riches and demoted poor Thomas from sainthood.

Each country had its own favorite pilgrimages, and in the spring the roadways were thick with travelers seeking the solace that

was reputed to come from visiting the Holy Places. In Spain, the people trekked to Saint John at Compostella, a Benedictine establishment. In Italy, they visited Rome for the blessing of the Pope and to view the five basilicas of the city.

But for the Norman overlords who ruled the Angevin Empire (which stretched from the Mediterranean to the northern parts of Scotland), one destination

Chartres Cathedral rises from the sand under the skilled and delicate touch of a master sandcastler. Its loneliness approximates the real cathedral which, from a distance, seems to rise in solitary splendor from the wheatfields of Beaune.

The soaring strength of the real cathedral lies in its flying buttresses, an architectural wonder that, alas, sand could not capture. The cathedral collapsed into an unrecognizable heap less than an hour after this picture was taken.

held absolute preeminence: the ancient shrine of Chartres.

Rising from the wheatfields of Beaune, today Chartres is but an hour's drive from the suburbs of modern Paris. However, in the days when the human foot was the main mode of transportation, it was several days away from the French capital and squarely in the domains of the Dukes of Normandy.

It had been holy from the time of earliest recorded history. The Druid priests of the prehistoric Celtic inhabitants of the area used it for pagan ritual. The Christianized Gauls and Vikings who conquered the area understood the aura of the spot and dedicated it to the Queen of Heaven.

The Cathedral of Notre Dame de Chartres (as it is properly called) sits atop a steep hill that itself sits inside an equally deep valley. The Cathedral seems, from a distance, to have been built on level ground. It is, however, built on one of nature's few naturally moated locations. Oddly, though, it has not been as heavily fortified as its location might suggest. That singular fact may be a measure of the re-

spect with which the shrine was endowed. The overlord of Chartres even had a peculiar title: He was not a duke, nor a count, nor a marquis. He was the Vidame de Chartres—because he was held to be the vice-regent on earth of Notre Dame. The last Vidame ruled his fiefdom in the seventeenth century during the reign of Louis XIII and Cardinal Richelieu, and figures prominently in Alexander Dumas' exciting novel on the Huguenot era, *Marguerite de Valois.*

A good measure of the piety with which these shrines were regarded is by Henry Adams in *Mont Saint Michel and Chartres.* He estimated that, during the century which saw the building of the Cathedral of Chartres, a billion dollars (equivalent) was spent on such houses of worship. In today's inflationary economy, that figure

might be closer to a hundred billion dollars! But Chartres could not be duplicated in today's world for any amount of money—except in sand.

The cathedral was begun in 1145, and the stone was quarried five miles away at Berchères-l'Évêque. The entire cathedral was cut from unusually hard granite in blocks of titanic size. It rose with feverish rapidity, but was the sturdiest building of its age and shows no sign of weakness even today, more than 800 years after the first stone was put in place.

But the pilgrims of the time would have told you that anything was possible with the Queen of Heaven guiding the work.

The ultimate pilgrimage for the medieval traveler was a trip to the real Holy Places—the Holy Land itself. It was, of course, this pilgrimage idea that created the Crusades, which were ostensibly undertaken to make the Holy Places safe for pilgrims.

Pilgrims were not a dour-faced, serious lot of travelers—quite the opposite. Pilgrimages in one sense were then what vacations are now: a change of pace, a change of

A second attempt at Chartres was planned after the untimely demise of the version on the opposite page.

But this noble attempt was even shorter-lived than the first. As solid as it looks, this Gothic splendor lasted only 30 seconds after the master

sculptors finished. After this one hurried photograph was taken, the entire edifice disappeared with a dull, almost noiseless collapse.

But even though this photograph is the only evidence that a sandy Chartres ever existed, the glory of the moment will live on.

This nineteenth-century reconstruction of Jerusalem shows the eclectic mixture of architectural styles that characterized cities of the Holy Land 2000 years ago. The Roman temples struggle to dominate the landscape, but the teeming heart of the city is covered with traditional multi-turreted Levantine structures.

scenery, a chance to meet new people (and perhaps a chance to indulge in a bout of vice here and there). One has only to look at Chaucer's lusty and outspoken Wife of Bath to know what vigorous adventures pilgrimages could be; she had been to Jerusalem four different times to "worship."

But whether they were recreational or religious, pilgrimages did have specific religious locations as goals. One of the most important then—as now—was the place of the Nativity, the little village of Bethlehem.

Bethlehem has always been an inconsequential town in every way but one. It was lazily fortified from time to time, but its only source of revenue for 3,000 years has been sheep-farming and subsistence agriculture. Its population, even today, is small.

But it was the City of David, and it is the location of an event that is

seen as the central point of history throughout the Christian world: the birth of Jesus. For nearly 1,500 years, time has been divided into years BC and AD, a historical division that gives enormous prominence to this scruffy hill village.

And Bethlehem's significance for Christians today is a particularly attractive one: it is a song of peace, of rejoicing, of unalloyed delight. What is more universally celebrated than birth? The other places in the Holy Land all have more somber memories: Calvary, the Holy Sepulchre, Gethsemane. And while the medieval pilgrim usually visited all the sites on a single visit, Bethlehem held a special joy for all.

To try to re-create biblical Bethlehem in sand might be to miss the point inherent in this small, dusty hill town in occupied Jordan. Despite the glories of the Church of the Nativity, Bethlehem

is a singularly unattractive town today, as it must always have been. It is scarred by unattractive signs and shops selling cheap religious articles, but even long ago it probably had no great charm.

The Bethlehem the world holds dear is not the dreary village of reality; it is the shining hill city of the sparkling Christmas message:

And, lo, the angel of the Lord came
upon them,
and the glory of the Lord shone
round about them:
and they were sore afraid.
And the angel said unto them, Fear
not: for
behold, I bring you good tidings of
great joy,
which shall be to all people.
—LUKE 2:9, 10

That Bethlehem—the Bethlehem of great joy and unlimited potential—is what pilgrims have always wanted to see. It has been the unhappy accident of a histori-

Bethle-
hem — not as it
was, but as it al-
ways will be in
the hearts of
Christmas chil-
dren. The city
walls, massive as
they are, seem
not forbidding,
but graceful. The
myriad little
homes and plazas
of the "City of
David" seem just
as they have
seemed for cen-
turies to armchair
pilgrims. And a
star of excep-
tional brilliance
twinkles
meaningfully
overhead.

cal irony that the actual village has been unimpressive and drab throughout the centuries.

And *that* Bethlehem is what was created in sand when a group of sand adepts set out to build an exceptional Christmas gift for the people of San Diego.

The idea of re-creating the physical Bethlehem as it really appears seems to have been rejected from the outset. What the Bethlehem castlers wanted was to create the Bethlehem that exists in the world's imagination: Bethlehem as it ought to be.

This was a Bethlehem that gave no portion of its attention to sorrow. Everything about it was focused on perfection, on peace, on beauty.

Technically it was a superlative maze of little streets, private homes, public buildings, soaring arches, and curving staircases. Its battlements were modeled after

the classic curtain wall that surrounded Constantinople in its heyday. Its intricately detailed nooks and crannies offered the viewer a nearly endless variety of new vistas, surprises, and delights.

Where is that stable? That manger? Those lowing animals immortalized in a hundred Christmas stories? The only hint was the massive blaze of light just out of view that might be the reflection of countless legions of fiery seraphim that guard a babe in swaddling clothes.

This Bethlehem was a model of planning. It was wired for electricity before the rough-cutting was begun, and many of the buildings and streets were lighted by their own individual pinpoint sources. The light cascaded down the byways of the town, poured out of windows, created long shadows on stately staircases. It was that

most unusual of sandcastles— built for night viewing.

Three sculpted kings moved slowly toward the main gate of the city, bearing costly gifts of gold, frankincense, and myrrh.

Bethlehem was created over a period of two weeks by a constantly changing guard of workers. Throngs of well-wishers surrounded it constantly during its construction. High school choirs scheduled concerts next to it; groups of schoolchildren visited and drew crayon pictures of it for their bulletin boards.

Though it resembled no city that ever existed in the real Holy Land, certainly it did not fall short of the city we all hold dear.
*The hopes and fears of all the years
Are met in thee tonight!*

Two views of Bethlehem show the astounding intricacy of this sandy labor of Christmas cheer. Built during December 1979 in San Diego,

Bethlehem attracted crowds of onlookers in the tens of thousands, as its creators worked for nearly three solid weeks to perfect it.

A city on a hill in this conception, Bethlehem was covered with staircases. The architects plotted walkways throughout the city, paths that traveled under hollow archways, up stairs, and through public buildings. The planning was so extensive that electrical wiring was buried within the city, and many of the larger buildings were illuminated *from within* by night.

7

Sandcastle Contests

Astartling blue sky arches over the sand and mirrors the warming depths of the ocean. Here and there a small cloud floats even higher than the tracks of jet planes, as though a celestial painter had daubed patches of white across a canvas of azure.

It could be Carmel, California: a perfect crescent beach surrounded by Monterey pines. It could be Galveston, Texas: a sandy island sitting atop Jean Lafitte's buried treasure. It could be Nantucket Island, or Mission Bay in San Diego, or any of hundreds of other festive communities across the country and around the world.

Beneath the palm trees at Mission Bay in San Diego, half a million people will congregate to watch the fantasies take shape. At Santa Barbara there will be a small-ish crowd of 50,000. Many a sunburn will sizzle this evening in the name of enchantment. And we have it on good authority that days spent sandcastling are days during which no aging occurs—they do not count against the time allotted to each of us. If all of us spent all our lives building sandcastles, we might well find immortality.

Sandcastle contests are like the meetings of witches' covens; they are thick with the spirits of the past, saturated with spells and unreality. The unspoken agreement between the contestants is that the world does not exist, that magic is the game of the day. Of course the whole experience is iced over with hilarity and grueling hard work, but the world of the preternatural is never very far away. And that is what allows the fantasies to come to life.

The eye of the sandcastler is fastened securely on the outrageous, the breathtaking, even the impossible. Sandcastle contests are an island of life where grandstanding is the virtue to be most cultivated. It is a day devoted to the art of the gasp, the gulp, and the giggle.

A deceptive air of solemnity pervades the beach before the starting gun is fired. Judges sip coffee at a crepe-paper-bedecked

113

Freestanding towers always impress even the most jaded contest judges. This Bavarian turret graced a winning entry at Laguna Beach, California.

stand as they review photographs of previous years' winners and exchange exaggerated remembrances of times past. Teams of contestants fill banks of buckets with salt water and divide the chores of the contest among themselves.

Sites are compared; the most level sites are eyed with the certain knowledge that graft has changed hands in the assigning of spaces. The weather is assessed; noses turn shiny white with zinc oxide ointment. Like paladins preparing for battle, the sandcastle chieftains keep their own counsels, summoning strength and fortitude for the event to come.

But the time, the place, and the overall appearance of the people on the beach give the lie to the long, serious faces. How can anyone be serious in that sunlight, that fresh air, and those baggy bathing suits?

The starting bell will sound and the frantic action will begin. Some time later a clarion shot will ring out and the shovels, the melon scoops, and the pie-servers will drop. Scowls will blanket the beach with, "If I only had another five minutes!"

The judges will tour the field in

their ribboned dune buggy, raising their eyebrows in an undisguised tease at each entry. Their score-cards will gather doodles and numbers, and a winner will emerge.

Trophies! Plaques! Wine! Cheers! The winners will rejoice all night, boosted ever upward by the adulation heaped on them. The losers will plan for next year and haul out the sun balm. And while the carousing is at its height and the joy is most abundant, the waves will creep up onto the beach of victory and wipe it out.

Why do it at all if it is so short-lived?

Because it's there. Because it's a release from the humdrum. Because it's a chance for 50,000 people to get together and work seriously at nonsense. Because it's a perfect excuse to eat under-cooked hotdogs with mustard, relish, and grit.

Because life is too short not to build sandcastles.

How can you care about winning in an event when everyone wins just by being there? How can you lose when the sky is blue, the water is warm, and the company is congenial?

F our views of a sweepstakes prize-winner from Mission Beach, near San Diego. One of the grand-daddy contests, Mission Beach attracts 500,000 spectators annually — and hundreds of entries.

This fantasy construction towered over the opposition. It is derived from an architectural style that still decorates much of the Netherlands. And it was built in less than four hours!

Precision sculpting is one of the most difficult roads to a judge's heart, but definitely one of the most effective. These austerely modern buildings speak of a future that is monumental in scope and execution. Perhaps the builders dreamt of a return to the glories of ancient Egypt. Their nearly mathematical perfection certainly praises the potential of technology, but it is surprisingly hard to envision people living here. An entry at Mission Beach.

Both east and west coasts are represented here — by way of three exceptionally festive annual contests. (1) Towers like these, built at Corona del Mar in California, might never have lasted through a real siege attack, but they won a prize in sand. (2) This hill city, also from the Corona del Mar contest, shows a highly developed sense of the type of architecture that wins: height is the single most impressive achievement. (3) This fairy-tale castle was constructed in the space of only two hours at Santa Barbara, California. Needless to say, it swept the judges' ratings. (4) Magnificently Martian in aspect, this superb drip castle with a hand-molded archway was a winner — at the annual contest held on Nantucket Island, Massachusetts.

116

1

2

3

4

Atranscontinental view of high achievement in sandcastling. (*top*) Reminiscent of the Tower of Babel or an Assyrian ziggurat, this soaring Mesopotamian wonder is from Bradley Beach, New Jersey. (*middle*) Galveston, Texas, saw the short life of this sprawling sand mansion, which seems to have a mini-White House on its upper terrace. (*bottom*) *Sic transit gloria mundi.* Even the finest achievements, such as this disappearing castle from Del Mar, California, are eventually reclaimed by the sea.

H ulk-
ing on the beach
like a refugee
from some dark
tale of dungeons,
this impregnable
château was
the creation of
sandcastlers
struggling for
the brass ring at
Solana Beach,
California. The
bravura aspects
of this sand
monument are
too numerous to
catalog: it's the
sort of castle that
chases the other
contestants off
the beach
entirely.

Prize-winning entries abound in technical grandstanding. (*left*) Staircases and arrow loopholes add to the feeling of authenticity of this entirely imaginary castle. Many judges make their decisions on detail work like this. (*this page top*) Cantilevered balconies make a convincing appeal from the standpoint of engineering merit.

(*this page bottom*) Holy Mount Saint Helens! And it's belching real fire.

As the sun slowly sinks in the west, the hardworking contestants drift off toward the post-contest revels, which are always substantial. Fatigue battles excitement, and a sense of ultimate satisfaction hovers over the group like the sun that warmed the day of glory.

Ah! The plans for next year!

8
Fantasy Sand Creatures

Fantasy lurks in the minds of us all. It may be a monster with a cockeyed leer ridden by a nude with flowing hair. It may inch its way across fifty feet of sand, all scales and folds.

Fantasy is as personal as a smile. One person's dragon breathes blue fire; another person's breathes orange fire; yet another person's dragon flies through the air and breathes no fire at all. Ask any three people to describe their own dragons separately and you will discover three different dragons.

Since there are no anchors to hold fantasy (there are no real dragons, at least none you can see at the zoo), all those fantasies have their own separate validities. Each one is, in other words, every bit as good as all the others.

One thing that fantasies share

from person to person, however, is their tendency to creep up unbeheld on totally unsuspecting victims. There is little time in the normal routine of daily business to devote to dragons. So when the dragons get to feeling too pent-up, they simply pop out and grab you.

How can anyone walk by such a creature unaffected? It may not be your own dragon, but it is, after all, a *dragon*—and a fairly uncommon sight.

Although fantasy is there in all our minds, it is not an easy task to summon it—unless you have some practice. And that may be where the beach comes in handy.

Even a novice can fashion a pretty respectable Jonas-whale from the sand. Even an all-thumbs all-around fumbler can put together a reasonable facsimile of a snake from Eden, a tortoise from Aesop, or—at least—a rabbit hole.

Children are the Grand Masters of imagination. They are also the only real authorities on sandcastles and sand sculptures. A child knows instinctively that dragons, knights, and monsters are real— yes, real. They are not parts of the physical world, but they are parts of the world of the mind. If dragons were not real, how could we recognize one on the beach?

123

Public libraries and art museums have always loved them. Children at zoos ogle them by the hour.

The lordly king of the jungle — the African lion — has been a favorite subject for artists from ancient times right up to the present. He appears here in two very different moods and two very different interpretations. (*top*) A realistic cat of monumental proportions in a state of repose. One presumes he's had a good meal recently, because there is a definite quality of kitty-cat in his demeanor. Santa Barbara, California. (*bottom*) A statuesque lion who might have been copied from stone. Every inch of this feline is regal. Although he is made of beach sand, he gives the impression of having been cast in metal: a study of form, masculinity, and power. Mission Beach, California.

The more realistic of the two lions vacillates between being dangerous and being playful, depending on how long you look at him. His mane is less carefully arranged and was created by the drip method.

Adults have forced themselves to live in a universe that is ever decreasing in size and space. They have forgotten, in most cases, how to pretend on a grand scale. One could be fairly safe in stating, for instance, that the number of dragons appearing to adults is quite small. The number of dragons appearing to children, on the other hand, is immense.

Fortunately there is a child hiding inside every adult, no matter how grown-up and crusty. Unfortunately, like all children, the ones

Once in a while, the whole beach seems to be obsessed with the same fantasy. These two representations of the "good life" both appeared on the same beach on the same day, but constructed by different sand builders. Perhaps with the grit of beach sand grinding your every move, you just naturally think about getting clean.

Here two gentlemen laze in their weekend bathtubs, soaking up the warmth of a San Diego sun. (*top*) A masklike grin graces this ecstatic fellow, whose face reminds one of a happy Halloween pumpkin. (*bottom*) This pot-bellied bather seems genuinely surprised by the tide which has grabbed not only part of his tub, but his feet as well!

hidden inside are adept at playing hide-and-seek. But if you listen closely, in the quietude of a beach at dawn, you'll be able to find the child within you.

Follow their swallowed laughs to their hiding places. Then bring them out into the daylight and watch them bring their joys, their playfulness, their innate imaginations to bear on that characterless sand.

No one but a child could possibly guess the wonders you will find.

125

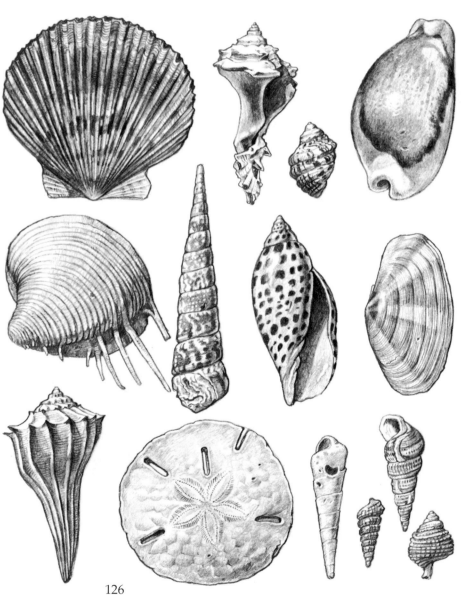

Arise, Lord Seashell!

If a lump of sand can be a castle, what glories are hidden in the real master builders of the sea! Cowries and conches build echoing vaults that hold the sound of the tide firmly in their inner depths. Scallops create fans worthy of Marie Antoinette. The legendary Nautilus surpasses the maze-maker of Knossos.

Countless creatures build their fantasy homes as shells — and shells seem custom-made for creatures of the sandcastler's fantasy. They become tile roofs, stained-glass windows, blazing medallions of heraldry. And the ultimate treasure of a living hermit crab is an ageless metaphor of a knight in shining armor. A primitive, fearsome reptile (*top*) charges out of the sand at Mission Beach, roaring and snapping at the passersby. The jagged, menacing teeth are, of course, seashells found at the site. (*opposite page*) Here's a snaggle-toothed Nile crocodile, who amazingly beached himself on Nantucket Island. His fearsome teeth are bits of broken seashell, and his scaly back is lined with row after row of scallop shells.

126

enizens of the deep are a major preoccupation of the festive sandcastlers at Nantucket Island. Here a fearsome crocodile basks in the summer sun, seemingly unaware of the odd growths that dot his back. The black sand was gathered at another section of the beach and used to give extra contrast to this Hook-chasing croc. Do you hear the ticking of a clock deep inside him?

One of the last great mysteries left to romantics and science-fiction addicts is the burning question of Nessie — the Loch Ness monster. Here a somewhat silly-faced Nessie pops up for a quick breather. Cautious as ever, though, the dreaded prehistoric apparition has stayed partially submerged in the sand, perhaps to facilitate a quick getaway in the face of danger.

No fantasy is too outlandish to be captured in sand. Here a reptilian winged gryphon poises momentarily on the beach of San Diego, its pterodactyl-like wings raised — ready to fly at its prey.

Another dinosaur survival. A nightmarish, gigantic lizard has burrowed

through the walls of a medieval castle — and is in the ghoulish process of devouring the inhabitants. A prize-winning entry in a Santa Barbara, California, contest.

The magic dragon below was a project at Mission Beach, California. It seems a little puzzled over the whole proceeding.

Storybook creatures abound on the beaches — and in the minds — of the world. Can anyone see a hooka-smoking caterpillar without being taken back to the Wonderland that lay on the other side of Alice's rabbit-hole? Here in a Disney-ish incarnation, the caterpillar is ready to blow smoke rings, asking the question: W-h-o a-r-e y-o-u?

A Cheshire Cat sits astride a couch (as any cat owner knows, the only place a cat can really call home). There is

nothing fuzzy or doubtful about this tabby's smile. It is squarely in the grand tradition of Wonderland.

Tump-tump. Pooh sits blissfully holding his beloved pot of honey, humming a hum. (His real name, as everyone knows, was Edward Bear, but the world knows him as Winnie-the-Pooh.)

Seaside communities can hardly ignore the lore of the ocean. A harpooned Moby Dick lies beached with the remnants of Ahab's whaleboat.

In the solitary fight of man against the cold, cold sea, a forlorn whaler floats free in an ocean of sand.

9

The Sands of Time

As you sit facing the ocean, with the sun on your back and the warmth of summer filling your soul, it is hard to believe that winter will ever come. Can the numbing heat of July turn to the blistering cold of January? Can New England's coastal greenery give way to driving winds and snow, and nature's annual vision of death?

Our world operates in cycles. Birth, life, death—and again birth, life, death. In the long view, every winter is the harbinger of spring. And as we are told in *Ecclesiastes*, "To everything there is a season, and a time to every purpose under heaven. A time to be born, and a time to die. . . . A time to break down, and a time to build up; a time to weep, and a time to laugh."

Just as the tree that dies in November blossoms again in April, the castle that collapses waits serenely in the minds of men for its rebuilding—another time, another civilization. Who can say that Camelot is gone forever? The legends of King Arthur say that one day he will return to glory, that he will rebuild the shining white walls of his city, and that his golden age will be upon us once again. Arthur's tombstone— wherever it may be—is engraved with the prophetic words:

Here lies Arthur,
the once and future king.

It is one of the hardest puzzles of life that destruction must precede prosperity, that the ashes of one life provide the sustenance for life to come after.

The sand in an hourglass holds a special fascination as it drips steadily toward the future. All of history streams forward in the same inexorable dribble—the rocks of ages no less than the sands in the hourglass.

It is with a sense of poignant sadness that we turn to the ravages of the tides of history. Crashing ruin and slow decay are the

133

apocalyptic horsemen of the hour, as the brilliant glow of the last bursts of sunsets glisten bloodily on the horizon and the deep indigo hues of night invade the sky.

The sandcastler sits with his back to the land, and watches his creation melt too quickly back into the level smoothness of the tidewashed beach. The children of the beach watch with desperation and horror, like the victims of a rabble horde destroying a city.

But the sandcastler has known from the beginning the fragility of his endeavor, and he watches the ending with as much fond joy as he employed to encourage the beginning. After all, the essence of a sandcastle is a predictably short life, a life cycle that can be watched from first to last in the space of a single day. It is like time-lapse photography, so compacted is the building and the destruction. The view from the beach is very nearly godlike, because the sandcastler's life span is nearly immortal compared to that of the sandcastle. So in a strange sense, sandcastles are an exercise in continuity and longevity, as the sandcastler realizes that a full life cycle can be made to take in so short a period of time.

Krak des Chevaliers
No prouder and no sadder monument to the ravages of time exists than the great heap of stones

known as Krak des Chevaliers. Stranded in the deserts of Syria, it rises like a gigantic sandcastle from the far reaches of history, mute and pitiful in its lonely isolation.

The footsteps of today's visitor to the Krak echo through the empty chambers that once resounded to the metallic clang of plate armor and the mellifluous drone of Gregorian Chant. The Great Hall is an empty place, fit only for desert vermin and small wild beasts. But once upon a time, it was a place of unsurpassed grandeur.

The Krak was built as the citadel of an order of crusader knights: the Knights Hospitaller of St. John. It is, without a shadow of doubt, the most perfect military castle ever built—and one of the most massive.

The inner castle was completed in 1170, despite the fact that two devastating earthquakes rocked the area during construction. The period of its glory was destined to be short, for it fell to the Sultan Beybars in April 1217.

As a physical structure, its proportions are nothing short of astounding, its conception and execution the pinnacle of castledom. And it is, though a ruin, remarkably intact. Its eloquent silence speaks knowingly of a time when holiness and barbarity were one, when unspeakable cruelty

and quiet saintliness went hand in hand.

The Krak was the jewel of the Norman Kingdom of Jerusalem, that peculiar hybrid nation established by the descendants of Vikings in what was thought to be the land of Abraham. It was itself a short-lived phenomenon, remaining a political entity for less than one hundred years. The Krak was the symbol of its heyday, a fortress that held absolute command of the Homs Gap—the only land route from the interior of Syria to Tripoli on the Mediterranean.

It is a labyrinth of baileys and passageways, all calculated to be the perfection of defensive architecture. And it is amazing that it ever fell, so well-planned are its fortifications. Its encircling plinth (called a *glacis*) is steeper than the great pyramids of Egypt, and allowed the base of its walls to be continually swept by the rapid-fire of murderous crossbows.

Its stone masonry is impeccable in every detail, each of the tens of thousands of granite blocks finished to a degree that would have satisfied the great builders of antiquity.

Its floor plan is actually a paradigm of simplicity: two rectangles, one within the other. The outer defense is the lower of the two, but even its walls defy description. The walls of the inner enclosure dwarf the surrounding

Ostensibly fought to recover the Holy Land for pilgrimages, the Crusades were brutal, murder-ous wars with only the barest veneer of chivalry. Broken and starving, two crusaders return home through the remnants of battle.

landscape. Fifteen feet thick at the top, and three hundred feet high, they look for all the world as if the were built by a lost race of giants.

The main entrance is a ramp of very wide, shallow steps, designed to accommodate processions on horseback. It bristles with defenses: a series of portcullises is the least sophisticated. There is one hairpin curve in the entrance passageway that is surmounted by a firing gallery that would mean instant annihilation to any surprise attacker.

As you enter the great inner courtyard, you see five delicately pointed windows and a Gothic doorway surrounded by five orders of decoration. That doorway leads into a fine gallery, and then into the Great Hall—an enormous cavern of a room nearly the size of a football field, and still completely intact. A prominent inscription on one of the pillars reads, "Take wealth, wisdom, and beauty, but trample on pride, for pride pollutes everyone it brushes."

Overshadowing all, the three highest turrets of the Krak stand guard over the blank southern wall, cascading hundreds of feet straight down. These three towers are the most massive in the citadel; even the arrow slits that pierce their walls are more than twenty-five feet long. Archers had to climb through them to take aim.

And yet it was breached. The final siege took only a month, from the beginning of March to the beginning of April, 1271. The walls of the gargantuan south face were mined, and caved in. In the place

After 700 years, the pride of the Knights Hospitallers stands in the deserts of Syria in a remarkable state of preservation.

It was built on the site of a series of castles that reach back through the dark corridors of history to the Egyptian Pharaoh Ramses II, who first determined that the site was strategically perfect. Later fortifications were built by indigenous peoples: Arabs, who called it Hosn es Sath (Castle on the Slope); and Kurds, who called it Hosn al-Akrad. It is from the Kurdish name that the unusual term, *Krak,* was taken.

The *glacis* slanting up to the inner curtain wall is steeper than the Great Pyramids at Gizeh.

Krak des Chevaliers fell to the Sultan Beybars in 1217 AD.

of that hole today stands a mammoth square tower built by the conquering Sultan, Al-Malek al-Zaher Rukh al Dunya wal din Abou al-fath Beybars. His historical name, Beybars, means "the panther."

And there it has stood, deserted, for the last 700 years. Now the domain of whistling winds, spiders, snakes, and small rodents, its glory remains. Its flying banners, ghostlike, reappear to the mind's eye at twilight. The clank of metal on metal resounds through its deserted halls. Mass is sung by the spirits of the dead. And 10,000 Moslem warriors rush through its mazelike corridors, slashing, killing, obliterating all.

Lovingly constructed in the image of the real Krak des Chevaliers, this sand replica emphasizes the desolation that befalls a castle that has failed to defend its inhabitants. As Shelley says in "Ozymandias," the lone and level sands stretch far away beside this colossal wreck.

Unlike the original, this sand Krak was built on an artificial *motte*-like mountain, giving the site the look of the Syrian original. Altogether, the height reaches over 7 feet; the circumference of the project was more than 10 feet.

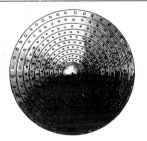

Château Gaillard

Seven hundred years ago the Angevin Empire was the most powerful political force in the known world. Its monarchs were French-speaking cosmopolitan adventurers whose possessions ranged from the Mediterranean to Scotland, taking in most of what is today France, all of England, and about half of Scotland and Ireland. Close relatives of the Angevin monarchs held tight-fisted control of southern Italy and Sicily (the Kingdom of the Two Sicilies, with its capital in Naples), the Holy Land (the Norman Kingdom of Jerusalem), and various other far-flung principalities.

During the last two decades of the twelfth century, the pinnacle of the Angevin Empire was a golden blond, muscular, chivalric giant: Richard Coeur de Lion (the Lion-Hearted). Myth and legend obscure our views of this commanding monarch, surrounding him with semi-real courtiers: Robin Hood and his band, Tancred, and others. The reality of Richard was almost more astounding than any of the stories told about him.

First of all, he was the most handsome, well-built, and charming man of his age. In a time when the average man stood under five and one-half feet tall, Richard was more than six feet. His hair and beard were the color of burnished gold, and he reputedly had absolutely no fear of anything earthly. His titles ran on endlessly: King of England, Scotland, Wales, and Ireland; Duke of Normandy; Count of Guienne and Gascony; Count of Poitou; Defender of the Holy Sepulchre; Duke of Aquitaine; Duke of Cornwall; Duke of Anjou—for a start.

He married the most beautiful woman in Europe, a princess from a tiny country between France and Spain: Berengaria of Navarre. And together they went to the crusades. Richard showed himself to be a man of his times in the crusades; he was a monster of cruelty to common people and a paragon of courtliness to nobles.

The enemy he faced in the field was none other than Saladin the Great, who matched him chivalric gesture for chivalric gesture. The two of them seemed in an endless competition for battlefield courtesy. They both survived, but Richard's less fortunate enemies died by the tens of thousands. When he captured Accra, for instance, he had the entire population of the city beheaded, even though they had surrendered to him. He simply hadn't time to bother with them.

On his way back from the crusades, Richard was kidnapped and held for ransom in Germany, where he became enamored of European politics. Being basically a warrior, his idea of diplomacy was to grab what he could and hold onto it. He was admirably successful.

His capital was in Rouen, France, and he protected it with one of the most amazing castles ever built: Château Gaillard. In a flash of warrior's insight, he selected a spur of granite that would command the entrance to his capital by controlling—absolutely—the flow of the Seine to the sea.

Here, where the river bends sharply and the valley of Les Andelys bows to the majesty of an unforgettable ruin, the crusader-king built what he thought to be a perfect castle, one perhaps modeled on the Krak des Chevaliers (which he had visited ten years earlier).

One of the most remarkable

Winding its way from the heart of France to the North Sea, the River Seine meanders by the ruins of Richard's masterwork, Château Gaillard. Richard saw Gaillard as a bulwark to protect his dukedom of Normandy from the rapacious French.

facts about Château Gaillard is that it was built in a single year. Its walls are ten feet thick. Its awe-inspiring moat was hewn from solid rock. It is sculpted so perfectly onto its ground that its walls—which surmount the living rock—seem to rise straight up to the sky from the river bed.

One year! In an age when a year's hard work was calculated to yield eight feet of height on a simple donjon! For a year Richard paced the construction site: commanding here, checking one of the magnificent ogive windows there, like a child.

They were a perfect match: the perfect monarch and the perfect castle. Although France is dotted with splendid remnants of

medieval architecture, few are more inspiring to visit than the ruins of Gaillard. Perhaps the shades of former glory are too strong ever to fade. Perhaps Richard and Berengaria will forever walk the castle's crumbling parapets, sneering southward at Paris, flinging insults from the mighty turrets at the river below.

And perhaps the angry souls of the thousands of soldiers, women, and children who starved to death in Gaillard still haunt it as well. Ironically, Gaillard—Richard's ultimate castle—lasted an even shorter time than the perfect Krak des Chevaliers.

Thirty years after the last stone was laid in place at Gaillard, the castle surrendered to a resurgent

French king, himself a reptilian horror who lived only for vengeance on the Plantagenets. At the beginning of the final siege, Philip of France magnanimously allowed the women and children of Gaillard to leave the castle grounds. But instead of letting them free, he penned them up within sight of the ramparts and starved them to death while their relatives watched. Horrors like that don't die just because the building is deserted.

The time to visit Gaillard is by night. The sounds you'll hear are only the wind, though they may sound like moans or screams. The flitting shadows are only clouds crossing the moon, or an occasional bat.

Towering over the Seine, the ruins of Château Gaillard speak, even today, of power and majesty. Once the site of unspeakable horror in warfare, Gaillard today seems a monument to Plantagenet military strategy — and to their sense of beauty. It is almost impossible to conceive of the frenzy of labor that constructed such a citadel *in less than one year*.

Nearly perfect in its amalgamation of a perfect natural site and the height of fortification, Gaillard was once admired throughout the length and breadth of Europe.

So much at one with its cliffside location, Gaillard could not have been accurately reconstructed on flat beach.

Here the sandcastlers of Torrey Pines State Park, California, hauled sand from the beach up to a rocky promontory overlooking the sea. Château Gaillard overlooks the ocean proudly, its defensive position intact. Even in sand, this Gaillard retains the majesty of its regal architect. It faces the tides with the heart of a lion.

Tintagel

Uther Pendragon was King of the Britons some time after the Roman legions pulled out of the islands for the last time. Much of our knowledge of King Uther and his famous son, Arthur, is contained in an ancient Welsh manuscript, the *Mabinogeon,* a work where myth and reality are treated as equals.

Some portions of the story seem undeniably real. There was an Uther Pendragon; there was a King Arthur. It is entirely probable that the two of them lived on a stony outpost like Tintagel, protected on three sides by the angriest seas that ever stormed against land.

They presided over the collapse of an entire civilization—a civilization that disappeared seemingly without a trace under the influx of the great Teutonic invasions of Britain during the Dark Ages. Successive waves of seaborne warriors washed over the islands: Angles, Saxons, Jutes, giving no quarter and sparing no Briton life. Arthur's last stand was doomed to failure before it started. Maybe that fact is what has made Arthur's name so glorious through the succeeding centuries: He knew he would fail, but his patriotism was too great to let him give up.

The story tells us first of Uther's infidelities in siring two children by two different mothers: one a human, the other a fairy princess. The son of the human mother was

Arthur; the daughter of the fairy princess was the evil sorceress, Morgan le Fey. As the fates would have it, neither Arthur nor Morgan knew of their kinship, and together they parented yet another generation: a warped, hating bastard named Mordred.

When King Uther died, there was a wailing and sorrow that covered the land, and Britain was without a monarch. Arthur, who had been reared away from the court by his father's wish, appeared to pull the great golden broadsword from the stone and proclaim himself king. Thereafter his magical sword, Excalibur, was constantly at his side.

He married Guinevere in a passionate love match that is only paralleled in history by the story of

Julius Caesar and Cleopatra: he growing older, she the very scent of springtime loveliness.

But unlike the faithful Cleopatra, Guinevere proved fickle. She began to cool her ardor after, it is said, five years of marriage to Arthur. And she fell hopelessly, fanatically in love with a young knight of the court, Sir Lancelot du Lac. Those two names—Lancelot and Guinevere—have burned their way through countless works of literature as the definition of adultery and illicit bliss.

But before Guinevere and Lancelot could tear out Arthur's heart, he created a court the likes of which even golden legend has never been able to equal elsewhere. The noble knights of the Round Table became the ideals of gentlemanly behavior and gallantry. The Order of the Garter was patterned on the Round Table when it was founded by Edward I.

Certain members of the Round Table have become symbols in their own right. The brawny-but-loyal knight was typified throughout the Middle Ages by Sirs Kay, Agravaine, and Sagramour; the perfection of courtly love as always by Sir Gawain. The essence of honor and personal commitment must forever remain Sir Galahad, in his unceasing quest for the Holy Grail. Sir Pelleas is the archetype of the unhappy husband with his Melisande. Sir Percival was thought to be the figure of physical beauty par excellence.

Crouching ruined among the rocky shoreline of Cornwall, the remains of Tintagel Castle give only a glimpse of what must have been great former glory. Massive in size and conception, Tintagel once protected these forbidding shores from marauders who may have been Vikings, pirates, or wild-eyed Irish. Traditionally thought to be the birthplace of King Arthur, Tintagel's origins are lost in the mists of early Cornish history. Can this be Camelot? Is this the site of the magic of Merlin? the evil of Mordred? the heart-rending betrayal of Lancelot? It is hard to imagine a finer place to dedicate to the memory of the man who pulled the sword from the stone.

Sirs Lionel and Bryan also figure prominently in several of the important Arthurian legends, and the number is rounded out by Sir Ironside, Sir Hector de Marys, and Sir Uwaine.

These titans of knightly lore lived in a great city on the Irish Sea, a great city long vanished and called *Caerleon* by its inhabitants. More recent legend has named it *Camelot*. Tradition has always had it that Tintagel Castle is all that remains. Arthur's mother, Igerne, was titled the Duchess of Tintagel.

The death of Arthur and the fall of Camelot has always been attributed to a coalition of evil forces. Lancelot and Guinevere robbed him of his happiness and his purpose. His illegitimate son, Mordred, turned traitor when he fell under the spell of ambition. And the invaders, led by fierce Teutonic chieftains, turned all to their benefit.

As great Arthur lay dying, he asked to be carried to the edge of a lake wherein dwelt the nymph, Viviane, the Lady of the Lake. He gave Excalibur, his sword, to his knights and asked them to drop it into the water. They were unwilling to do so and hid the sword instead. Arthur asked them what had happened when they dropped the sword into the lake. "Nothing," they replied. He knew they were forswearing themselves and told them to go back and throw the sword in the lake. This time they did as they were told. Before the sword could drop into the water, a beautiful white arm reached up from the surface of the lake—Viviane herself—and gently took the sword from the hands of Sir Lionel.

When they reported this to Arthur, he knew they were telling the truth. He lay back and died.

It is said that Arthur waits in one of the heavenly spheres for the day of his return to reestablish Camelot. Since his name means *bear* in Latin, it has been said that his sign is the constellation of the Great Bear (the Big Dipper). As long as those stars shine down on us at night, we can rest safe in the knowledge that one day Arthur will return.

143

Our revels now are ended. These our actors,
As I foretold you, were all spirits and
Are melted into air, into thin air;
And, like the baseless fabric of this vision,
The cloud-capp'd towers, the gorgeous palaces,
The solemn temples, the great globe itself,
Yea, all which it inherit, shall dissolve;
And, like this insubstantial pageant faded,
Leave not a rack behind. We are such stuff
As dreams are made on, and our little life
Is rounded with a sleep.

THE TEMPEST
Act IV, scene 1

Camelot is one of very few magical places that hovers between myth and reality. It is the castle of countless dreams.

This Camelot fantasy may bear little resemblance to Tintagel, but it shares a concept of greatness, of splendor, of heroism with all the tales of Arthur and the Round Table.

This is the castle where Uther Pendragon courted the beautiful Igerne, Duchess of Tintagel. And to them was born a boy who would remain in the hearts of men for thousands of years, the symbol of the Golden Age past and to come.

Towering 12 feet above the beach, this Camelot was the loving product of seven sandy Merlins, who labored two days to create this enchanting splendor.

And every one that heareth these sayings of mine,
and doeth them not,
shall be likened unto a foolish man,
which built his house upon the sand:
And the rain descended,
and the floods came,
and the winds blew,
and beat upon that house;
and it fell: and great was the fall of it.

MATTHEW, 7:26-27

Text: Joe Allen
Design: McQuiston & Daughter, Inc.
Photography: Marshall Harrington
Editors: Rick Harmon, Gayle Kidder
Illustrators: Richard Carter, John Dawson,
David Diaz, Denise Hilton-Putnam
Production Art: Carol Freese, Laurie Miller
Typesetting: Boyer & Brass, Inc.
Lab Assistants: Roy Davis, Byron Pepper,
Nancy Samuelsen
Photographers and Agencies:
Aerofilms Ltd.
Mary Allen
M.N. Breitenbach/Photophile
Larry Cronin, Nantucket
Michael di Persio
James R. Hommes
J.D. Mickelson/Photophile
L.L.T.Rhodes/Photophile
Tom Tracy/Photophile
Toni Wasserberger
British Tourist Authority
French Government Tourist Office
German National Tourist Office
Italian Government Tourist Office
Romanian Government Tourist Office
Spanish National Tourist Office